I0473512

How I Teach

Reflecting on fifteen years in
design education

Brown Bear Publishing
1408 Cotton Street
Austin TX 78702

© 2017 Jon Kolko. All rights reserved.

No part of this publication may be reproduced or transmitted in any form or by any means, electronic or mechanical, including photo-copying, recording, or any information storage and retrieval system, without permission in writing from the publisher. Details on how to seek permission can be found by emailing Jon Kolko at jkolko@gmail.com.

How I Teach

Reflecting on fifteen years in
design education

Contents

Introduction

When I was 24, I was looking for a career change. I found a job at the Savannah College of Art and Design (SCAD)—a large art school in Savannah—teaching industrial design and interaction design. I got the job in June, and would start teaching in September. I had three months to prepare to teach four classes, and I was panic-stricken. I had no idea what to do.

The extent of my teaching experience at that point was being the teaching assistant in a class in graduate school, where the curriculum was set and the professor told me what to do—which mostly consisted of grading multiple-choice tests. My classes at SCAD were to be in a variety of design specialties, like information design and product form development, and there was no one who was going to tell me what to do. I was on my own.

I felt overwhelmed, and so I had a conversation with an existing faculty member at SCAD, Bob Fee. Bob offered me two things, both of which turned out to be what I needed to get started.

First, Bob gave me advice: he told me to treat the creation of a course like a design problem. That meant sketching it out visually, testing it, and most importantly, iterating on it—treating the course plan like a work in progress, rather than a finished artifact. This advice helped me see that I would probably be wrong with my first attempt at a curriculum plan, and being wrong was okay. The pressure and anxiety I had about teaching was that I worried I wasn't going to get it right or be good at it. By thinking about it like a design problem, I realized that "being good at it" wasn't as important as "trying and iterating."

The second thing Bob gave me was much more tangible. He gave me his lesson plans. He gave me syllabi, lectures, notes, sketches, student work examples, and all sorts of other digital artifacts. And he gave me his blessing to use them in any way I wanted—to borrow (or steal!) generously as I developed my own courses. This meant that I was able to learn by example—by exploring how he broke down complex topics into simple ideas, how he threaded a narrative through a ten week quarter, how he thought about grading, and the types of things his students produced. I wasn't going to be teaching the same classes as him, but it didn't matter. These materials became the backbone for my own content development.

And so I worked to develop content and curriculum for my first quarter teaching, agonizing over each class and sketching, erasing, and revising my own plans. And then the first day of class was upon me. I remember standing up in front of the class, introducing myself, and—scared to death—kicking off the quarter.

I didn't do very well. For all my planning, my classes weren't well structured, I didn't have confidence in my own teaching abilities, the students were skeptical of a new professor, and I felt all over the place teaching four classes (and close to 70 students) at a time. But I got through it, and over time, I got better. I learned from my experiences, and to my surprise, students were forgiving of my mistakes. They felt that I was on their team, and my shortcomings in the classroom were ignored as I slowly built their trust.

I worked at SCAD for close to five years, and in that time, I taught over 500 students. I built curricula in both industrial design and interaction design, I mentored undergraduates and graduate students, and I learned to teach.

After I left SCAD, I was able to apply my experiences at a number of other educational institutions, such as at the University of Texas at Austin, the Center for Design Studies of Monterrey, in Mexico, and Malmö University, in Sweden. And then, in 2007, I started my own school called Austin Center for Design (AC4D).

I started a school for a variety of reasons. One was that I saw a need for low cost, high quality graduate-level design education. Design graduate programs in the US can cost as much as $80,000, which is outrageous. I wanted to develop a school with comparable quality, but at a fraction of the cost.

I also wanted to develop an educational program that was focused on a unique form of subject matter (interaction design, design strategy, and social entrepreneurship), topics that weren't broadly taught and that I felt had strong demand.

And, I wanted to develop a program that combined what I had learned at my various teaching experiences, but without the organizational and bureaucratic roadblocks that I had encountered at some other institutions.

Many of the faculty that taught in those first years of AC4D were new to teaching. I tried to duplicate what I gained and learned from Bob. I gave my educators the same advice (to treat curriculum design like a design problem), and I gave them my course plans, too.

AC4D has turned into a well-recognized and respected school. Our alumni have gone on to do great things, and our education process has become more and more refined. But, we've always treated the curriculum like a work-in-progress. We reinvent the classes, make changes, and constantly iterate on our course plans.

Throughout my experiences at SCAD and AC4D, I've seen new teachers struggle, for many of the same reasons that I struggled. Teaching seems overwhelming, and the responsibility of being an educator makes even simple tasks feel daunting. What if I get it wrong? What if I teach them the wrong thing? Will I ruin their careers? Will they feel misled, or that they didn't get their money's worth?

The "new teacher" problem is amplified in recent years because there are an increasingly large number of adjunct teachers entering academia. Adjunct teachers are more cost effective for large universities, because the schools can do crappy things like avoid paying them health insurance or regular salaries. These adjunct teachers are often thrown into the deep end with little or no background on the course they are to teach, and little training in how to teach it.

That lack of training goes for tenured professors, too. Many tenured professors are employed because they are experts in their field, not experts in teaching. When I talk to tenured professors, some describe that teaching is more intimidating than their research, because they've had literally no instruction on how to manage or structure an educative experience.

In addition to adjunct and tenured professors, I also see a proliferation of corporate facilitators—of people responsible for organizing and running training within a company. These people are tasked with introducing complex topics, like design thinking, into the fast moving and chaotic machine of business. And, again, they may have little or no experience teaching. They are experts in their field, but not necessarily experts in education.

Even "plain old designers" are starting to feel the pressure to teach. Our role as designers is increasingly that of facilitator—of bringing both users and clients along for the creative ride, and helping them see the benefits and value of various forms of design methodology. It's not enough to do great design work and come unveil it to an audience. Instead, our role is to teach other stakeholders about what it is we do and why we do it.

An influx of teachers, but no real plan to teach them how to teach— that's recipe for disaster. I want to help change that. In all, I've had over fifteen years of experience teaching design. I'm a good teacher, but it took me a long time to get here. As I reflect on my own path, I realized that I have a lot of things I've learned that can help other teachers—to help adjuncts, tenured professors, corporate educators, and design facilitators. I can make their path a little easier, and can help improve the quality of education in a broad sense.

This text is what I've learned so far. It's about design education, but it's applicable to other fields, too. It's for people responsible for building curriculum and designing classes, for people who are in positions to teach, and even for students who are thinking about how their own courses are structured and run. I hope the material is actionable: it's material I wish I had when I started.

Course Plans

A class starts with a plan. It's a framework for the experiences students will have: it describes what sort of learning will take place, how it will take place, when it will take place, and why it will be valuable. Before I start teaching—well before, often even months in advance—I start putting together that plan. The plan itself includes the strategy of the class and also the tactical methods, assignments, and student interventions that occur through the educational experience. The act of putting together the plan serves as a way for me to role-play that educational experience to see what it "feels" like.

Building your first class can be daunting. Curriculum design is an entire profession. People go to school just to learn how to build effective and strong courses. But most of us don't have the luxury of working with an instructional designer, and instead, we're left on our own to shape the classes we teach. As I described in the introduction, building a new course is like working through a design problem. If we treat it as less precious and less finite, it becomes more tractable.

So, just like in a design project, let's think about how we can frame the problem of curriculum design and break it down into pieces and parts. The plan is made up of a few sections: course outcomes, a schedule of classes, a series of grading opportunities, and a course description. Let's take a look at these in more detail.

COURSE OUTCOMES

An outcome statement is an assertion, or promise. It's something that a student will have learned, gained, practiced, exhibited, or demonstrated as a result of completing your course. Outcome statements are measurable. There is a way to view, count, compare, or otherwise judge the student's progress towards attaining the outcome. Course outcomes may look like this:

As a result of taking this class, students will:

- *Be able to model complicated systems and services through the use of diagrams*

- *Be able to quickly sketch ideas for interfaces by hand*

- *Be able to communicate through sketching, both in a formal capacity as well as in a real-time, facilitation style*

- *Be able to quickly iterate through interface design, using input from real users to inform decisions*

Each outcome statement is self-contained and focused on a particular skill, concept, or idea. For example, one outcome is about interface visualizations, another on system and service modeling, and so-on. Each outcome stands alone.

Each outcome statement is measurable, and well-structured outcome statements can be measured by looking at the things a student makes. For example, the outcome statement about visualizing interface ideas through hand-drawn sketches can be measured in a variety of ways:

Was the student able to visualize ideas quickly? This can be assessed by keeping track of how long it takes the student to draw. Were they faster at the end of the course than they were at the beginning? Were they as fast as a concrete benchmark (for example, 10 sketches an hour)?

Were the student's ideas realistic? This can be assessed by looking at what the student sketched to identify if it can actually be built, or if it is based on a sound set of assumptions. Were the ideas technically infeasible to build? Did the ideas come accompanied by explanations to justify their realism?

Was the student able to use hand-drawn sketches? This can be assessed by looking at the mechanism the student selected to create the interfaces. Did they use paper and pen, or did they jump right to a digital tool like Adobe Illustrator?

A semester or quarter-length course typically has 3-5 outcome statements. A larger number of outcomes becomes harder to assess, and teaching towards so many outcomes can feel watered-down or shallow.

Creating the outcome statement

To create my course outcomes, I start by identify the things I want a student to know how to do. I don't worry about wordsmithing the perfect outcome statement; I just list the skills that, when the course is over, I want the student to have. Design is a practitioner field, and when students graduate, they should have a set of practical real world skills. So, whenever possible, I try to capture specific *active skills*—things someone can *do*—instead of simply passive skills—things someone can *know or feel*.

This often takes several iterations. For example, in crafting the outcome statement "Be able to quickly develop realistic ideas for interfaces using hand-drawn sketches", my first few iterations may look like this, in order:

Learn to think about sketching
Learn to sketch
Learn to sketch quickly
Sketch quickly

Learn to think about interfaces
Learn to sketch interfaces by hand
Learn to sketch interfaces by hand, quickly
Sketch interfaces by hand, quickly

There's an evolution to these outcome statements, moving from passive ("think about sketching") to active ("learn to sketch"), to simply describing the skill ("sketch")—removing the "Learn to", and focusing on outcome instead of the method.

Identifying ways to achieve outcomes

Now that I've identified the outcomes, I identify the ways a student can attain those outcomes. I list as many of these as I can. For example, to sketch an interface quickly, a student might:

- Trace an interface with tracing paper

- Sketch a simple copy of an existing product interface

- Draw the components of an interface, like buttons, sliders, and so-on

- Sketch as many interfaces as they can in a set amount of time (such as an hour or over a week)

- Compare and contrast two products that do the same thing, such as two music playing apps, and draw the differences

Each of these activities could be an in-class activity, an assignment, or even an examination; they are things that produce an artifact, and then that artifact can be judged.

Teaching to the outcome

Now, I think about how I can teach the concepts behind each of these activities. For example, to sketch a simple copy of an existing digital interface, I need to teach students to:

- Select appropriate interface elements, such as radio buttons, check boxes, and so-on

- Establish criteria for what makes a "good" interface

- Draw using different line weights

- Emulate areas where padding, margins, and whitespace create a sense of composition

- Consider and realistically sketch the size of type

These become the things I teach—the content of the class itself.

The role of outcomes

So, to recap, we:

- Identified a learning outcome ("Sketch interfaces by hand, quickly")

- Identified a way for students to arrive at that learning outcome ("Sketch a simple copy of an existing product interface")

- Identified content that I need to teach ("Teach students to draw using different line weights")

With each step, we're moving away from things the student does, and towards things the instructor does.

These outcome statements serve three core purposes.

First, **outcomes act as a guide for students**. They indicate what a student can anticipate learning in a class. This sets expectations, so students can prepare for a certain type of learning experience. When students know what they are going to learn, they can better contextualize that learning as it happens. I urge students to revisit the outcome statements (that I've identified on the syllabus) throughout the course. This helps them reflect on their own progress—they can see, throughout the duration of their learning experience, if they are gaining the skills and methods that I've articulated.

Additionally, **outcomes act as a guide for me**. They help me determine what course content is relevant and what types of learning interactions will be most effective. As I make curriculum decisions, I can ask myself, "Does this particular activity or content support those learning outcomes?" If the answer is no, I can rethink my planning to better serve the students.

Finally, **the outcomes act as a form of handshake between me and my students**. They become the agreed-upon boundaries for the class. They serve as a definition of value: I agree to teach to that value proposition, and students agree to learn from it.

SCHEDULE OF CLASSES

Now that I know what I have to teach, I can create the course schedule—the things that happen throughout the course. This schedule includes details around the course dates, content themes, in-class exercises, out-of-class expectations, and when assignments are due.

Content themes are the topics that will be addressed during class. These relate to the outcomes. For example, if an outcome statement focused on visualizing ideas quickly, course themes may be centered around idea visualization: concepting, rapid ideation, sketching techniques, and so-on.

In-class activities describe what a student can expect to experience when they are in class; these include discussions, presentations, and other activities. By listing the items a student will encounter, students can set expectations about the demeanor and tone of the class, and they can come prepared to participate in each unique type of educational interaction.

Out-of-class activities describe what a student is required to do when they aren't present in the classroom. These typically include course readings, homework, and group discussions. By listing these items, students can manage their schedule to ensure that they are prepared for each individual meeting time.

Assignment due dates are important to list so a student can structure a methodical, thoughtful, step-by-step approach to their course output. These artifacts act as the core assessable items, and so students should be able to best plan around producing quality output.

Drawing the timeline

To build the course schedule, I first sketch a long horizontal line on a large sheet of butcher paper. I put a hash mark for each class session; if there are two classes a week for 8 weeks, I draw 16 hash marks.

Next, while keeping in mind the course outcomes, I look at the things I need to teach and try to assess how long it will take me to teach them. In our example above about learning to draw digital interfaces, I need to teach students to *draw using various forms of line-weight*. I think this will take two classes—one to start to learn about becoming comfortable holding the pen and making marks, and one to learn about pressure and different forms of drawing tools. I'll draw a bar that spans the two classes, creating a simple Gantt-style visualization of time passing.

To decide that this would take two classes, I imagine (role-play) what I will cover in each class, and how students will respond to it. My inner dialogue sounds something like this:

What does it mean to get comfortable holding a pen and making marks?

They'll need to see an example from me, hear me describe how to do it, but most importantly, they'll need to practice. I can imagine them drawing lines, and then circles, and then trying more complicated things like coffee cups. They'll need lots of practice. Since classes are two hours long, I expect them to draw for almost 3.5 hours.

Now, I'll pepper in the various in-class and out-of-class activities that I want students to experience as they begin to build towards a given outcome. My goal is to highlight progress and show how one set of learning activities leads to another, and how students slowly build mastery of an idea through exploration, practice, and assessment.

This is an iterative process of planning. I'll cross out components and redraw them, work backwards to re-evaluate my methodology, and even question and recast the outcome statements. I use big paper and a sharpie because it emphasizes that the curriculum is in-flux—it's not done yet, and I can freely change things. I also use big paper so that I can get a sense for the whole even while focusing on the details. I've found that jumping onto the computer in a tool like Excel or a project management tool like Smartsheets forces me to be myopic. When I work on the computer, I'm less likely to completely abandon an idea, start again, or treat my ideas like drafts.

GRADING OPPORTUNITIES

Eventually, I become comfortable enough with the timeline structure I've drawn and the outcomes I've identified to think about assessment opportunities, which are places where I can grade the student's progress.

Grading opportunities are places where I can see if a student is showing competency in a given area. This might be a natural stopping point in an ongoing project, a written essay, a formal test, or a design exercise. It doesn't mean it's the end of the road—I believe in having more, but smaller grading opportunities throughout the course. This gives students a chance to correct their behavior if they aren't doing a good job or aren't learning the concepts.

Let's stub out where grades may live on the course schedule. This means defining where those key grading interventions make the most sense.

Earlier, we dedicated two classes towards learning how to hold a pen and making marks. As a result of these two classes, I want students to achieve the outcome statement we defined:

Be able to quickly sketch ideas for interfaces by hand

So, after those two classes, it seems like an appropriate time to insert some form of assessment to see how they are progressing towards that outcome. I'll add an indicator to the timeline that after those two classes would be a good time to have an assignment due.

I discuss assessment in more depth later in this text, but for now, simply adding the assessment moments to the timeline is enough.

COURSE DESCRIPTION

Now that we've worked through outcomes and a schedule, let's author the course description.

A course description acts as the short mission statement of each class.

It reads as a value proposition by declaring what students will learn, framed as a promise. Authoring the course description is hard. Like creating the schedule and the course outcomes, this is an iterative process of writing and editing. The goal is to create a two or three sentence summary that succinctly articulates the mission of the class. That means it captures everything we've discussed above, in a summary fashion.

For example, in a class focused on creative problem solving, the course description might read:

This course teaches methods of creative problem solving and ideation related to interfaces, including sketching, diagramming, and the underlying approaches of abductive thinking and divergent thinking. Students learn how to quickly visualize ideas, iterating through variations, and allowing an idea to evolve quickly and effectively.

The language used sets up a series of commitments to the student. They will learn methods (and the methods are named); and they will achieve goals (and the goals are named). Just like the outcomes, the purpose of the course description is to set up a frame around the course, acting as an objective container in which we can make course decisions. For example, given that frame, it wouldn't make sense to teach theory—that doesn't fit within the container of the class. It would make sense to teach drawing, though, because that supports the commitment of visualizing ideas.

In larger schools, a course description is often the only clues a student gets as to what is taught in the course; prior to the course beginning, they may not be able to view a full course plan. That means the description needs to be specific. Here is an example of a bad course description:

Course Description: This course teaches students to draw. They'll learn about drawing and how to do it. At the end of the course, they'll be able to sketch.

Unfortunately, I've seen course descriptions like this. It's too vague; it doesn't give students the ability to understand what they will be gaining as a result of taking the course. What will they learn about drawing? What does "be able to sketch" mean—be able to sketch in a certain style? In a certain medium? To a particular level of skill? There's no clear delineation of boundaries, and so a student is left to make their own inference about the course content. It's unlikely that their expectation will align with the professor's course plan, making it difficult for them to be successful in the course.

PUTTING IT ALL TOGETHER

Here's a summary of what we've done to arrive at a course curriculum.

1. We wrote outcome statements

2. We identified what a student would do in order to achieve the outcome

3. We identified what we would teach in order to help the student achieve the outcome

4. We sketched a timeline for the class, assigning durations to our course content

5. We stubbed out places to assess progress at natural stopping points

throughout the course

6. We wrote a detailed course description that helps a student understand what they'll learn by taking the course

This is a good starting point for our class. But I can't emphasize enough that course planning is fluid. Before class begins for the quarter, I'll revise my course curriculum as many as twenty times. There's no pressure to get it right on your first try.

At some point, we run out of time—we can't iterate on the course curriculum anymore, because class is starting! At this point, I'll capture my course plan in a syllabus. While I emphasized iteration on the course curriculum *before* class starts, I try very hard not to change the curriculum *after* the class begins, because it's not fair to the students. In some schools, the syllabus is referenced as a "contract between the teacher and student." This is a little stuffy, but I think it has the right intent: it says that the student and professor agree that these concepts and ideas are important and will be taught in a certain style and order. Students can plan their time, and their expectations, based on the document you create.

The syllabus has exactly the same elements as the course curriculum, just written in a simple and easy to understand format. It lists the course description, outcomes, and grading criteria. It may also include things like office hours, assigned readings, and other course policies (such as how you want students to hand in their work—via email, dropbox, etc).

Foundational Skills

I've built several academic programs at different schools, and each was unique. Some focused on design strategy, and included classes in ways to shape corporate vision, while others were grounded in industrial design fundamentals (like making beautiful objects). But they've all shared common types of skill development—common design subject matter that I feel should be part of any design program (and probably any educational curriculum at all). These subjects include contextual research, design synthesis, service design, product management, and usability evaluation. For me, these are the new "foundations"—the things that act as the bedrock for any type of design education.

Let's look at a way to structure each of these topics in your own curriculum.

CONTEXTUAL RESEARCH

Perhaps the most important skill we develop is contextual (or observational) research. I teach one of the core tenants of user-centered design: observing real behavior in order to influence design decisions. Students learn how to structure a research plan around a particular focus area, and then perform ethnographic research with real people.

This form of primary observational research has several key benefits.

Observational research helps students realize that the people who will use their creations are not like them. They may come from a different socio-economic background, have different ideals and values, behave in unique ways, and most likely, they don't think about design. By observing people in the real context of their real work, students come to understand and respect these differences. The differences help shape assumptions during a design phase. As students develop empathy with people, they become more and more confident making decisions that represent these users. They can act as a proxy for the users, channeling and championing their perspectives, wants, and needs throughout the process.

Observational research helps identify opportunity areas where design can make an impact. Students identify places where workflow breaks down, where errors creep into a process, or where someone is dissatisfied with an existing product or service. They hear first-hand about areas where an existing design is frustrating or difficult to use, and observe people struggling to achieve their goals. These are very well-structured design problems: there is a problem, and the student can now fix it. In school, this is useful because the structure of the problem itself acts as the preliminary design frame or constraints in which to solve it.

Observational research identifies more ambiguous opportunity areas. Students may start to *feel* that there is a place where design can help, but the problem is not as well defined. In these cases, qualitative research helps them better shape an argument for a thematic problem (such as "workflow doesn't make sense" or "people are angry about customer service") instead of a specific problem. These opportunity areas are often more valuable to a company, as they indicate areas for disruptive innovation.

Observing real behavior also has the added benefit of getting the students to leave the safe confines of the studio and go explore the world. It's tempting for students to hide in the building where things are predictable and in their control. But user-centered design demands that they go to the users and observe them, building a sort of apprenticeship relationship with the users.

When I teach students about contextual research methods, we spend time learning about good interviewing techniques. Students learn not to ask closed questions that provoke yes or no response ("Do you like this?"), and instead ask questions that lead to more discussion ("Can you tell me your feelings about this?"). We investigate the differences between leading questions ("You don't like this, right?") and neutral questions ("How does this make you feel?"). And, we discuss how to bring a demeanor of curiosity to a problem space. The student may have knowledge about the research subject matter, but they learn to check that knowledge at the door and come to the research ready to learn.

I teach students to develop a research plan that shows their research focus, who they will talk to, where they will find these participants, and a script of what they will say. They iterate on this plan several times to ensure it makes sense. Most importantly, students role-play the research scenario. They act out what the research will feel like, so they can adjust their research script accordingly.

Students also learn the mechanics of conducting research. I have students audio-record each research session. They learn to prepare their recording technology (does the recorder have batteries? is storage full?), to organize their note-taking materials, and to ensure that they understand the roles of each teammate. They learn about informed consent (explaining to a participant ahead of time what they can expect from the study, and what compensation they will receive as a result of participating), and prepare informed consent forms.

When they actually start conducting their research, students run into some common problems.

Getting access to participants is difficult. It may be impossible for students to gain direct and in-context access to specialized roles, such as an air traffic controller or an army general. We discuss how this mirrors the realities of a professional research study, and that in both an academic context and a professional context, they will need to learn to think critically about the situation and propose a result. They learn to use "next-best" research participants, such as a retired army member or someone involved in airport operations instead of flight control. These proxy-users may be more readily available, and will still give students valuable information that they can use to better understand a topic.

Students also run into a problem of wanting to craft the perfect research plan. They agonize over the details of their script and research focus, iterating on it over and over. Group members struggle to make decisions, and so they spin. But they don't realize that in many respects, their focus and plan doesn't matter. These things act as a starting place for research, but the research itself guides and steers both the conversation and the subject matter plan. It takes practice to feel comfortable with this fluidity. It's my role to help them move forward—often, to nearly push them out the door to get started.

Contextual research skill development recasts how students think about research. Instead of performing secondary research, like cursory web searches, or conducting questionnaires and surveys, students learn to research with real people. I think this fundamentally changes how they approach problem solving because they are able to form an empathetic connection with people. This is valuable not just in a creative design profession; it's valuable in every context where research plays a role.

DESIGN SYNTHESIS

Another foundational skill that I include in my curriculum is synthesizing data and information. As students conduct research, they generate a large amount of raw data. By itself, this data isn't very useful. It isn't actionable and doesn't help the student move forward with their creative design process. Students make sense of that data by interpreting it; they learn to make sense out of the data. Synthesis is about making informed inferences, leaps from raw data to insight. This is a hard skill to learn, and students are taught several different methods to help them make sense of the data they've gathered.

First, students learn to create diagrams. There are a number of formal methods that they learn, such as *design workflow modeling* and *concept mapping*. No matter the method, each technique shares some qualities:

- **Students need to draw their ideas, rather than talk about ideas**. They learn that making visual models helps them mange the complexity of relationships between pieces of research data. It's hard for us to hold lots of intersecting and sometimes competing ideas in our heads at once. Externalizing the information through diagrams makes it easier to see connections between data. Students can say "I saw this happen over here, and you saw that happen over there; what if there's a relationship between those two things?" I encourage students to sketch their ideas as diagrams, even at the most rudimentary level of fidelity. I'll frequently provoke students to "stop talking and draw."

- **Students make sense of data collaboratively, instead of by themselves.** Students are encouraged to work in their teams as they progress through the mess; working in a group offers multiple perspectives on any given data, allowing for more broad interpretation of that data. When there is a visual sketch drawn on the whiteboard, students can modify it as a team. It isn't precious; it becomes a shared way to make meaning out of data.

- **Students develop models that they can use for further design.** A diagram isn't just a communication mechanism. It can be "used" during further design phases to understand how a new idea will influence the model. For example, students may work together to build a model of the behavior they saw during research. Once that model is created, it describes the existing state, capturing existing behaviors and activities. Now, students can introduce new ideas into the model, and see how those changes impact behavior. Can they make someone's life easier? Can they change the way a system works? The model becomes active, rather than passive—it's "used" to craft new ideas, just like a hammer is used to bang a nail.

In addition to making diagrams in a synthesis class, students also learn to develop insights. An insight is a provocation, a statement about human behavior. It makes an assertion, and then it acts as a scaffold to judge future design ideas. If a student is exploring the topic of banking, they may write an insight like "People have a hard time saving because they only think about purchasing decisions in the short-term, rather than the long-term." They build that insight based on their research and diagramming, and I encourage them to state it with confidence.

This synthesis process is a new way of thinking for students who have been taught that you need "all of the data" before you can move forward. I want them to learn to move forward with just enough data, moving as quickly as possible towards a hypothesis.

Student consistently struggle with synthesis. It feels overwhelming, and it's hard to see progress being made during the process. Ambiguity is frustrating. It takes time to arrive at insights, and students feel as though they are wasting time and spinning their wheels. I believe that any interpretation is valuable even when there's no obvious forward momentum. But in the moment, students don't see that. It's my job as a facilitator to help them see why diagramming and exploring insights are valuable, and that they are making progress.

Often this means synthesizing *with* them, instead of coming in and evaluating what they've already done. I'll get into the weeds, sketching diagrams and provoking new insights. Students see how long it takes to marinate in the data because they can watch me spend a large amount of time with each group.

Students also struggle because they don't know when they are done. There is no right answer, and so synthesis could go on forever. They don't have the experience to see when they've worked through ambiguity to arrive at simplicity. It's my job to help them see that. I do this by leveraging their visual models and their insights in order to sketch new ideas, solutions, and innovations. I create new design ideas in front of them, sketching how they would work and how they would help people. I make the connection between their synthesis efforts and my ideas obvious, and they can start to emulate how I use their sensemaking structures to drive creativity.

Synthesis is a fundamental skill that all students should learn. It's how we make sense of the world around us—it's a form of active sensemaking that integrates new knowledge into existing worldviews. And it's the backbone of critical thinking and decision making.

SERVICE DESIGN

Another foundation skill students develop in my classes focuses on service design. Service design is about experiences that happen over time. In our service design class, students learn to think about problems as parts of an ecology—that when people encounter something that's been designed, that something is part of a larger system. More specifically, students learn to show how a person interacts with a service over time, and then to show how different parts of a service come together to foster positive experiences.

Our life is made up of services. When you travel, your airline provider is offering you value through a service (the ability to get from here to there). When you go shopping, the grocery store is offering you value through a service (the ability to purchase groceries).

In both examples, the service is made up of many touchpoints—places you interact with the service. When you travel, you interact with a website, a kiosk, a mobile phone application, a gate agent, a flight attendant, an uncomfortable seat, and so-on. Each of these contributes to your overall experience.

By learning to think about and design services, students gain a deep understanding of two core ideas. First, they investigate the interconnectedness of things. Nothing exists in isolation, and our relationship with the world is impacted by the context of our interactions. This is an important principle to learn in order to deal with and manage the increasing complexity of a technology-centered world.

Next, they begin to think about the world as a series of interactions and experiences, rather than objects and artifacts. Services rely on interactions with people, and to think about the world through this lens is a form of empathy. Students need to think about people and learn about what they do, say, and feel. They then learn a diagramming technique called journey mapping to understand the relationships between those physical, digital, and human touchpoints. This mapping style can be used to illustrate both the problem (or existing) state of a service, as well as the ideal (or future) state of a service design.

To build a journey map, students start by thinking about the end-to-end experience a user has as they achieve their goals. Students observe a local business, like a hair salon or restaurant, and begin to consider the role of each person involved. What does the employee do? What are their responsibilities? How does their sphere of influence change as the day and their shift progresses?

Students also consider the various products people interact with during the experience. Does the server use a point-of-sale tool? What about handling customer's credit cards, or the food itself? These artifacts represent points of interaction, places where designed artifacts show up. Each of these elements could be designed in isolation, but that wouldn't support the larger ecosystem of the customer experience.

Students pay attention to both the spoken and unspoken policies that govern what the people in the system can and can't do. They look at rules and procedures. They note power influences, such as a relationship between management and waiter, and also self-imposed policies, like showing up for work on time.

When they're done, they've developed a tacit understanding of the system. They have the benefit of a "birds-eye view"; they are able to see what all the players in the system do, and can leverage their omniscience to begin to propose new changes to the system.

In addition to learning about how a person experiences a service over time, students also learn to dissect a service into atomic parts. Using the same case study of a local business, students extract out key components related to information flow, the environment, and the power dynamics between actors in the system.

Increasingly, businesses and governments are building services rather than simply focusing on products. They recognize that they can provide value to their customers and constituents by focusing on human to human interactions. In learning service design skills, students acquire the methods and vocabulary to craft strong services.

USABILITY EVALUATION

One of the key components of my curriculum is usability testing—teaching students how to evaluate their work to see if it makes sense to other people, and to see if they can use it effectively without encountering errors. When students first start to make things, they have a hard time seeing their creations from the perspective of another person. They think, because they understand it, someone else will too. This is a form of "expert blindspot." Usability testing sheds light on places where the expert blindspot (or, simply lack of experience) has led to poor design decisions.

I teach two main forms of usability testing. First, I teach a method called Think Aloud testing. This is a simple technique: have a person use a product to try to achieve their goals, and have them talk out loud while they use it. It's a simple technique, but there's more to the method than meets the eye. By talking out loud while accomplishing a task, a person is articulating the contents of their working memory. As long as the facilitator doesn't prompt them with queues that lead to introspection, the talking gives a great view of how the participant thinks about the new design.

Queues that lead to introspection would look like this: "Why are you doing that?" or "What did you expect to happen there?" It's tempting to ask these questions, but participants can't answer them effectively. Introspection changes the contents of working memory - it alters how the participant actually goes about solving the problem.

So, during the evaluation, students simply prompt the user to "please keep talking" if they fall silent for more than a few seconds. This ensures a continual stream of comments, and gives students a very clear view of where their designs are hard to use.

This form of testing can be done with any fidelity prototype, even hand drawings on paper. When students are designing digital products, like websites or phone apps, they prepare each screen in a flow on a different piece of paper, and swap the screens out one at a time as the participant points at various elements on the paper. We practice in class. It takes a fair amount of organization prior to running an evaluation like this, because students need to prepare each screen and then place them in an order where they can easily and quickly reach them. By running a "test of the test" with other students, they can become more familiar with the test methodology itself and with their prototype materials.

I've noticed that some students are reluctant to show their design to a user if they don't feel that it is perfect. I help them see the benefit of constant (and early) testing by reinforcing how quick a change can be made during early stages of design. When a design is still a marker sketch on a sheet of paper, changes can be made simply by crossing things out. This is a cheap and fast way towards improvement, and when students realize how much time it saves them to test early in their design process, they embrace this form of testing.

In addition to think aloud testing, students learn a second, supplementary form of testing called Heuristic Evaluation. While think aloud testing requires end users, Heuristic Evaluation is a form of expert review. Students compare their interface to a series of best practices, identify places where it doesn't comply with these practices, and propose changes based on the misalignment.

Heuristic Evaluation relies on design principles that are well established in industry. Some of these focus on the same types of problems identified by think aloud testing, things like language misalignment or lack of help and documentation. The benefit of Heuristic Evaluation is that it doesn't require users, which makes it a faster technique to learn and practice. Students simply inspect what they made and compare it to the heuristics. It takes less time, and identifies a number of usability issues.

However, the method alone fails to identify major cognitive misalignments in a design. It doesn't typically identify large navigation problems that confuse users. It also doesn't help students hear about how users think about their interface, so students may be less likely to take the results seriously. There's something really impactful for students to see an actual person struggle with their design. It resonates on an emotional level, students are more likely to make changes to their work when they observe real people.

Usability testing can be done throughout the curriculum. It can be performed any time the student has made something. As part of our user-centered curriculum, I encourage students to test early and often and include testing as a regular part of their process.

PRODUCT MANAGEMENT

Our curriculum also includes foundational instruction in product management, and I consider it fundamental to how students learn about professional design practice. Product management is the set of skills that bring a product to market. It's about developing meaningful insights into human behavior, crafting a product vision, identifying product/market fit, and managing a product roadmap.

We already saw the importance of teaching synthesis to students. Product management leverages those synthesis skills. First, students develop actionable, meaningful insights. These insights come from translating design research into provocations about human behavior. Students interpret their research findings, ask "why", and identify connections and themes they see emergent from what people do and why they do it. An insight is an assertion. It describes how people are or want to be, and generalizes from a small set of participants to a larger population.

For example, if students were exploring the topic of school debt, they may have conducted research with college students. During the research, perhaps they noticed that one participant was piling up student debt notices, unopened; another was repaying their loans only haphazardly and irregularly; and still another was using their loans to buy food and other things that aren't related to school. Through synthesis, the student may have identified a theme around irresponsible behavior, and then interpreted that to mean that student loans were surrounded by a context of fear. They made an inferential leap that the participants they observed were acting irresponsibly because they were afraid of confronting such an insurmountable amount of debt.

Based on their research, this seems plausible. And so, while synthesizing the data, they arrived at the insight statement: *"Students are afraid of debt, and that fear drives them to act irresponsibly."*

There are several important qualities to this insight. First, it builds on the research that the students conducted. There's a narrative thread that can be tracked from the insight back to the discrete observations from their research, and that gives them the ability to tell compelling stories that support the insight. Next, the insight is presented as a fact. Even though research was only conducted with a small set of participants, the student makes a sweeping generalization about the whole population of college students. This inferential leap is important because it acts as a provocation. This is where innovations come from—these inferential leaps identify and point to problems that can be solved.

Now, students can begin the process of sketching and exploring designs that will help their participants become less afraid of their debt, and act more responsibly about paying back their loans. Their insight creates constraints, which free the student to explore with more confidence that they are solving a real problem, a problem worth solving.

Once the students have developed insights, we start to build a product vision. This is the solution to the problem; it's the way to fix the problems identified by the insights we've built. Students go through a divergent and convergent ideation process. First, they develop as many different ideas as they can in order to explore the problem space. They produce new innovations that build on their insights. For example, now that we have an insight that "Students are afraid of debt, and that fear drives them to act irresponsibly", our students can brainstorm as many ways as possible to help the participants they saw become less afraid of debt. They might come up with new products that show how consistent payments now lead to a shorter debt lifespan, or help students set goals for saving each month, or show them how changing lifestyle activities (for example, drinking cheap local beer instead of expensive imported beer) can give them the money they need to make their loan payments.

We come up with as many ideas as they can. We use a variety of forced provocation methods to help students explore non-traditional, unexpected ideas. For example, I may prompt them to identify solutions that include a vehicle, or a pet, or a restaurant. These are things not typically associated with college debt. This form of strange provocation encourages them to make extraordinary leaps, finding ways to connect things that aren't normally connected. It helps them move through the obvious ideas, into the realm of the absurd, and then, from the absurd into the innovative.

As a result of divergent thinking, and over the course of several weeks, students develop hundreds of different ideas. They sketch them at a variety of levels of detail. Some ideas are just written words on a piece of paper, while others are sketched as comics, showing how someone will use the new product to achieve their goals.

Then, we begin to converge, and this introduces the idea of "product/market fit." Students need criteria to assess the ideas they've developed. Insights were developed by purposefully making leaps from a small amount of data towards a statement about a whole population. We moved from talking about only a handful of students to talking about all students. That's critical for presenting an opportunity area, but it doesn't ensure that the opportunity will be adopted by the market. That's where product/market fit comes in. Students learn to analyze the opportunity from a variety of market lenses to see if there's an audience for what they've created.

For each of the divergent ideas, students identify a total addressable market, which is the maximum number of people that can benefit from the idea. This gives them a sense for ideas that can have broad appeal. To understand how big the market is, they'll need to conduct secondary research, and think critically about who would actually use their product if it existed.

Next, students identify the ideas that are technically feasible. Their ideas need to be built, and if that requires a substantial investment in technical infrastructure, the idea won't resonate for some time. For example, if their idea requires micro-loan payments, but the loan repayment system isn't set up to handle payments like this, the road to implementation will be long and arduous.

Then, students look for ideas that are politically and socially feasible. Ideas are constrained and governed by laws and social norms. These can shift, but shifting them takes time. We coach students to think critically about their ability to make these changes, and to judge their ideas accordingly. For example, they may identify a new design product that makes it easy for students to file bankruptcy paperwork in order to purposefully default on their debt. But, there may not be a legal way for this idea to succeed (in the US, you can't bankrupt out of student debt)— and changing the law would be a difficult process.

As a result of examining the total addressable market, technology feasibility, and political and behavioral feasibility, students narrow their potential design ideas to a more manageable subset. I encourage them to down-select their ideas to two or three. And then, they create a vision narrative. They develop a scenario that walks through how a user will use these new product ideas to achieve their goal. This vision narrative starts in writing. It's a story, with the user moving step by step through the system. Quickly, we move to a sketched scenario in a comic style. And then, students develop a realistic product vision. Their student debt application will come to life and will look real. And this can be tested using the evaluation methods we discussed earlier.

Students have developed insights, crafted a vision, and identified product/market fit. The last piece of product management is developing a product roadmap. Even though students sketch a product vision that's comprehensive, in a professional environment, it would be built in stages. A roadmap shows the sequence in which new capabilities will be added to a product. It's a timeline that introduces a logical approach to new feature definition. For example, if students need to log into a system, the log in feature needs to be built towards the beginning, probably before advanced features are added.

The product roadmap forces students to add realism to their idea and to prioritize the most important pieces that fulfil the value proposition and deliver on the idea's core benefit. Producing the roadmap is iterative. We treat it like any other deliverable; students build the roadmap, we critique it, and then they iterate on it.

Product management is a relevant skill because students will inevitably be building digital products. The world is a digital place, and even human-centered services will likely have digital product touchpoints. Students learn take a value-focused approach to product management, so they are prepared to build new ideas in a realistic manner.

The Design Studio

Now that we've built a class, and explored the foundations of a design curriculum, let's look at where a class gets taught—in one of the most unique parts of a creative field, the design studio. A studio is a special place. It feels alive and full of energy. A studio usually has sketches and ideas all over the walls, diagrams on whiteboards, natural light, and big, open spaces. It's not just a physical place, though. It's also an attitude. A studio culture is one that values creativity and when you enter a studio, you feel a creative "vibe." It feels different than a typical office that may have a fleet of cubes or conference rooms, or a typical classroom that may have rows of desks. It feels more like a space of exploration rather than a space of "finished ideas."

A studio is also an educational structure, or a way of learning (sometimes called pedagogy—a fancy word for "teaching style"). The unique qualities of a studio that we'll explore support the unique nature of learning about creativity. Design education is experiential. The studio exemplifies experiential learning.

The idea of a studio as a learning model is usually new to students. It's not something familiar, because most grade schools and high schools focus on a "butts in seats" model of teaching, where students sit in desks and watch a teacher at the front of the room. Because it's a new way of thinking, students need to learn how to behave in a studio. They may be used to having an assignment, working on it by themselves, and then handing it in to be graded. This is a fairly linear process: I work, I complete, I get graded.

But that's not how a studio project works. In a studio, learning is much more organic. Students may have a brainstorming session around a whiteboard, and then break off and sketch individually. Then, they may come together, critique the work, and draw on top of each other's sketches. A professor might give them feedback, and then they may present their work. This process is fluid. It can feel unstructured, and some students don't know how to manage that lack of structure.

The professor adds structure.

THE ROLE OF THE PROFESSOR

In a design studio, knowledge is produced, not disseminated. That's a subtle but critical and foundational point about design education: In a design studio, the professor does not *have the knowledge*, and their role is not to *give the knowledge* to the students. Instead, the student develops the knowledge through various forms of inquiry, action, reflection, and conversation—all intended to help them look at a problem in a new way.

My own education was rooted in a studio culture. But when I became a teacher, I forgot some of the ways studio worked. I felt like I had to have all the answers. I felt a pressure to appear as an authoritative source; I was nervous that the students wouldn't take me seriously if I wasn't seen as all-knowing. But instead, I found that students were more receptive if I took a role more akin to a guide. I needed to recast my expectations of myself—that, instead of being an expert, I needed to view myself as a facilitator, partner, and mentor. This is someone who has had a certain quantity of creative experience and who can anticipate, during the knowledge-generation process, where various patterns, methods, approaches, or techniques will be most effective.

Perhaps the most important part of a studio environment is the relationship between the professor and the student. It's a unique relationship grounded in the traditional apprenticeship model of learning. Simply, a student learns alongside. They ask questions, try things, and when they make poor decisions, they are corrected in the moment.

Let's look at how a studio class is structured to help build that master/apprentice relationship.

INTERACTING WITH THE PROFESSOR

My studio classes begin with a brief group meeting with the whole class together in one place. We discuss the general progress each team has made since our last meeting, and review our project schedule. I try to keep this meeting to a short period of time, often as brief as 15 or 20 minutes.

Then, I transition the class to a work session. Students are instructed to focus on their projects (usually in teams, as most work is collaborative), and I begin to circulate through the studio.

I meet with each group individually and ask them to show me what they've developed since the last time we spoke. The actual artifacts they've produced drive the conversation—they pin up their work and they point at various decisions they've made. Instead of speaking theoretically or generally introducing concepts, the learning is grounded in the things the students have made. That means the student needs to come to class prepared to talk about these artifacts. It seems obvious, but I need to teach them that they have to actually bring the artifacts to class. Since many students haven't experienced a studio before, it's important to set the rules. I tell the students that they need to come prepared with their work—that it's *fundamental that they bring an artifact, not just an idea*. And, they learn that it's their meeting, which means they not only need to be ready to discuss and analyze that work, they also need to have a list of tasks that they want to accomplish or questions they want to ask.

As we meet, we move fluidly between looking at their work, sketching on the whiteboard, discussing the decisions they've made, and making real-time changes and explorations. I'll offer my own opinions and participate in iterations alongside of them, often sketching directly on top of their work.

The expectation for a student is that they participate in the conversation, sketch new ideas, and take notes. Because studio classes are unique and many students won't have experienced them before, I need to tell them these expectations, particularly the part about taking notes.

I'll prompt students: "This seems important. Do you want to take a second and write it down?" Additionally, since I want students to habitualize making things instead of talking about things, I'll also prompt students: "Can you show us?" or "Why don't you draw that?"

As I work with the students, and design alongside them, I provide a commentary about what I'm doing and why I'm doing it. This helps students see how I make decisions. They can compare how they would have solved the problem with how I solve it, and in that respect, they learn both specific design practice (these are the steps I take to move forward) and also generalized design methods (these are the tools I use when I do my job). For example, a group of students are working on designing a service and they may have sketched a simplistic diagram on the whiteboard, at a superficial or vague level. I can iterate on that diagram to make it more useful, adding directly to their sketch. As they watch me draw, they may hear me say:

The initial sketch does a good job of showing the high level flow through the service. Let's add more detail. I'm going to break the structure into phases, here's phase one. We'll call that the discovery phase. Most services start when someone learns about them, often from another person. Let's put a placeholder there to remind us that we need to conduct more research about that part. Then, I'll move on to the other phases. Why don't you take the marker, and add phase two: I think it should be something about learning, where the user begins to understand the value of the service. What's a word that captures "learning" most effectively?

My instruction has several key components.

- **I take over.** I see that the students are working only at a vague level of detail, so I begin to show them how detail matters. Instead of letting them drive, I realize they are struggling and I take a more "command and control" approach to the conversation.

- **I leverage my experience**. I fill in the blanks on their rough diagram with more discrete elements, and so students see that their original sketch was too broad. I also add a phase called "Discovery", based on my understanding of how services work. They wouldn't have thought to add that; I lean on my own experience to show that part.

- **I write and draw directly on their work**. It's not effective to simply talk about changes they need to make—they need to see me actually make those changes in the context of their own work. This helps them see my suggestions in more fidelity, and most importantly, it helps them realize that work is iterative and that what they've produced is not "precious."

- **I discuss what I'm doing as I do it**. I offer a running commentary of why I'm making the decisions as I make them, so that students can understand my intent and the thought-process of my decision making.

- **I transition so the student is in charge**. When students see forward momentum through my actions, I transition the role of "being in charge" back to the group. This helps them claim ownership over the ideas, even if I'm the source of those ideas.

In addition to working through problem solving with the team, I'll constantly prompt them with the question "What problem are you trying to solve?" A design problem has so many facets that it's easy to get overwhelmed. Identifying a specific problem to solve helps narrow scope, and makes a large problem seem less insurmountable. And, clearly articulating "this is the problem I want to solve" helps the team remain aligned. I urge the team to write it down, and to constantly revisit the statement.

Doing it right

I've noticed that students become very concerned with checking with me to make sure they are "doing it right." They see my expertise as a check on their work, as if I need to bless what they've made as being correct. This is particularly true for inexperienced students, who want to make sure they are following directions, or doing exactly what I, as the professor, want. It's hard for them to learn that, in design, there's no *right*—there's only *better and worse*. I take a specific-to-vague approach to helping them learn this.

At the beginning of the curriculum and course of study, I give students painstaking parameters that describe what my expectations are. I'll specify the number of sketches to create, the font to use, even the size of paper to draw on. I contain the creative space as much as I can, and I'm prescriptive to the point of minimizing creative exploration. Counterintuitively, this gives students *more* room to explore, not less. By excluding decisions, they can focus. If they have to use a certain paper size, they don't need to spend time worrying about what paper to choose. If the "rule" is to only use Helvetica, they don't need to explore different fonts. Instead, they can drive their attention towards the goal of the assignment. They can isolate that goal.

I write these constraints down in the assignment sheet (I'll share more about how I write assignment sheets later). When students ask me in these early classes if they are "doing it right", I refer them to these constraints. They are free to deviate, I explain, but their client (me!) has specific needs, and if they don't meet them, they better have a good reason. Some students will ignore the constraints anyway. During critique, this gives the group a chance to discuss the nature of client or stakeholder expectations. I use a simple way of explaining the importance of meeting those expectations. If a client asks for a blender design, I explain to the students, and you give them a toaster, the client is unhappy. But if you give them both a blender *and* a toaster, you have a happy client. You went above and beyond, and they see how committed you are towards meeting their needs. The rules that I've spelled out in the assignment sheet are the blender. Meet the rules first, and then, if you want to explore outside of them, build the toaster.

I'm very prescriptive when students begin their studies. Over time, I become less and less specific. My grade sheets will become vague, and at some point when students have progressed to an advanced level, I won't hand out grading criteria at all. Now, the answer to "am I doing it right?" needs to come from the student themselves. They need to identify constraints (often emerging from the work itself) and then use these constraints to shape their exploration. They need to structure assessment criteria, and seek out criticism. This is a transfer of responsibility. The professor isn't in charge of the design work anymore. The student is.

The reason I become more and more vague is because design problems are inherently ill-structured. Every single problem a student will encounter as a working professional will have ill-defined and often conflicting requirements. Their job is to make sense of ambiguity and find clarity among the mess. No one will be there to tell them what to do and how to do it, and to help prepare them for this, they need to become comfortable making their own rules. But this only works because they experienced having the rules drawn explicitly for them early in their education. They've learned what it means to add structure to a project. They've learned that they need to isolate elements, add boundaries, and work within constraints. Once they've learned this, they can apply their own constraints in later exploration.

TEAM DYNAMICS

Projects in my studios are nearly always in groups of two or three. A well-structured team learns to work together fluidly. They trust one-another, and so they can focus on their design work instead of focusing on interpersonal problems. But frequently, personalities clash within a group. Students who don't have experience working in a group struggle. These are some of the things they struggle with.

- **A conflict of communication style.** Some people are direct and blunt. They communicate their judgement and observations in a no-nonsense tone of voice, and don't curate their language to deliver bad news in a good way. This is at odds with other students, who both give and expect feedback to be more supportive. "That isn't working" and "There are a number of parts of this that are just so good, but when they come together, I don't think it's doing the best job it really could be" get to the same point, but do it in very different ways. When these collide, there is tension.

Sometimes, this stylistic problem is present in something as simple as inflection and volume. I had a student who had a very loud voice, and some of the other students in his group felt that he was yelling at them. They interpreted this as antagonistic, even though his intent was collaborative.

- **A conflict of perception of roles.** Some students want to lead and view themselves as an autocratic leader—someone who determines a direction, makes decisions, and ultimately is in charge. Other students view a team as a collaboration, where no one is in charge and decisions are made through consensus. When there are multiple "leaders" emerging in a group, forward momentum become difficult because each individual feels that they own decision making. This results in debate, conflict, and sometimes, shouting. When there are *no* "leaders" emerging, the group spins. It's difficult to find a path forward if no one can commit to a direction, and so this leaderless group considers multiple paths over and over without ever making a decision.

- **A conflict of work ethic.** Some students dedicate more time to their course work than others. When the effort gap becomes noticeably large, students begin to feel resentment towards one-another. That resentment splits the group, where students begin to work individually rather than collaboratively. Sometimes, the wedge becomes so strong that students end up with individual designs instead of a group result.

- **A reliance on old skills.** Students come to school with a set of existing skills. It's tempting in a group project to fall back on those skills. For example, if one student is skilled in sketching, and the project requires sketching, they become the de facto "sketcher." This means that no other student will get to experience and practice that skill, and the "sketcher" won't have an opportunity to try new methods.

In all of these cases, the solution is frequent and honest conversation. Ignoring the issue makes it grow. Constant intervention through conversation heads off a problem before it becomes too large to manage. These problems are all present in professional work as well—they don't go away once the student reaches the working world, and in some cases, the problems become magnified by corporate hierarchy. Students learn, through collaborative projects, that constant communication is critical for making team-based decisions and managing a productive group dynamic.

This communication doesn't happen naturally for students, and I often need to spark the dialogue. During a studio course, instead of simply discussing the quality of the work, I can discuss the quality of team dynamics, and force issues to come to the forefront. This is most effective by being direct with observations. If I see participants working individually instead of collaboratively, I may say something like "I see that each of you are working individually. This means you are missing out on collaborative value, like idea sharing, group brainstorming, and the tacit knowledge a student brings to the group. Why don't you join the group over here?"

But it's not enough to simply tell the students what to do. I need to show them. Because in many cases, they don't actually know how to improve or change. If they are working individually, and I want them to work in a group, I can show them what group work looks like. We can gather around a whiteboard, and I can facilitate a group conversation. If someone is excluding another teammate during the conversation, I can call attention to that. And I can hold a meta-conversation of how we are working together, so students see and experience through example how to shift or change their behavior.

A studio is about purposeful introspection and retrospection. I prompt this reflection. I ask students to think about how they feel about a given situation, and hold a structured dialogue about the student's feelings and reactions. I ask things like *How did this activity make you feel? Why do you think you felt this way? In comparing how you feel to how another student felt, why do you think you had different reactions to the same experience?*

These questions force even further introspection and cause deeper thinking. They act as provocations for students to explore their feelings and their actions. Many students feel as if they are the only one who "doesn't get it" or "can't do it", and to hear that their peers are also struggling helps to reset their own expectations about their own behavior. In this way, introspection and retrospection act as tools of comradery, which in turn help to create a collaborative learning environment.

STRUCTURING TIME

A design studio is typically long. Some run as long as 8 hours. This helps instill a work ethic in students who are likely used to much shorter, burst-style learning. Design takes time, and to achieve a sense of flow and depth, students need to focus on their work and achieve creative flow. The duration of the studio says "creativity requires dedication" and helps students build a muscle memory of expectations around how their work evolves and changes.

A design studio also helps students develop their own pace of learning. In a given studio, they may meet with their team, meet with the professor, take breaks, and work independently. These mirror the types of things they can expect when working professionally, and so they learn how to culturally approach a design problem—they learn a cadence for design exploration.

Because studio projects are self-directed, students need to establish their own timeline. I act as a guide, giving them a "strawman" of when things should be done, but I leave them to the task of project management—of building a calendar and revising that calendar over the course of the project. Many students have never created a to-do list, never planned a schedule beyond a few days out. I teach them how to create a to-do list at an appropriate level of fidelity, breaking things into achievable tasks. Over time, they learn to self manage the project. The act of project management helps them "own" the success of the project. When they see that they are running out of time or falling behind, it's up to them to reconfigure their schedule to better hit deadlines.

STRUCTURING THE SPACE

While the studio is an attitude and education model, it's also a place, and the dynamics and shape of the place impact the way students use the environment. The space belongs to the students, not to me, and that means they have to feel as though they can take charge of it. They need to be empowered to change the space as their needs change, and so the "rules" of the space need to be flexible. And, the physical parts of the space need to be changeable. Here are some of the keys to a dynamic workspace for students.

Perhaps the most important part of their entire space is that students "own" it—they feel they can permanently take control of a portion of the space and customize their area. That owned space doesn't need to be large. It can simply be a desk and a chair. But it signals to the student that they have control. This is important, because I want them to feel in control of their work, too. Instead of asking me for guidance with projects and assignments, I want them to make their own decisions, even when these decisions aren't great.

Having their own space and the ability to customize it tells the student "you are in charge." It's important that they hear that over and over, so they stop assuming there are invisible rules that will mandate what they do and how they do it. If they want to change the orientation of the desks, they should have the freedom to do that. If they want to bring in a fridge, or a microwave, they are "allowed to"; in fact, I try to remove all rules entirely. If they feel that the space is theirs, they will be more likely to spend time in it.

In order to reinforce to students that the workspace is theirs, I give them free access and large responsibility. All students have keys to the building, so they can come and go at all hours of the day. And, simple tasks like ordering coffee or taking out the trash are left to the students. This isn't laziness on my part. Instead, it further says to the student that this is their space and they need to self-organize to take care of it. And they do self-organize. Typically, one or two students will begin to pull together the other students to take care of simple chores or to prepare the space for class.

A dedicated workspace means that students can pin up their work and leave it there. As a design project grows, students produce more and more artifacts. They reference these artifacts throughout the process of synthesis and ideation, and so they need to spread out. An interesting part of sensemaking is the relationship between physical space and ideas. When someone places an artifact in a space, that physical space becomes a shortcut to the idea. Simply by glancing at a particular area of the desk can trigger thoughts about the artifact that's placed there. If the materials are constantly removed, that sensemaking is short-circuited. There's no "muscle memory" for the area of an idea, making it hard to dive back into work after a break.

In addition to a dedicated workspace, design studio should have space suitable for pinning work up as well as a large number of whiteboards. Pin-up space is important for both formal and informal critique. My classroom walls are covered in a material called homasote. The material takes pushpins easily, and can be painted and repainted; it's also fairly inexpensive. Additionally, I place as many permanent and rolling whiteboards as I can within the space. This indicates to students that they should be externalizing their ideas and working collaboratively whenever possible.

Some of this collaboration is purposeful, such as in a group project, or including their peers in casual conversation about an assignment. But equally important are serendipitous meetings of students, late at night, where they reflect on the nature of their studies. I've overheard these reflective conversations, and they often are deeply introspective. Students show their vulnerability to one-another. They'll describe their frustrations and their passions, and start to realize that their concerns and fears are shared by their classmates. This form of conversation rarely comes from a scheduled meeting. Instead, it's shared when students have their guard down, often after working hard on a problem and making little or no progress.

Class Interactions

The design studio is a place where students learn experientially with the supportive guidance of a professor. Class time in the studio is one of the most important parts of design education. It's a structured opportunity for students to interact with me and to interact with each other. It's also rare: some programs have as few as 5 hours of professor/student facetime per week. Since it's so important and so infrequent, I try to use the time as effectively as possible by leveraging different class styles, including exercises, critique, presentations, and dialogue about theory.

EXERCISES

In-class time can be used for exercises that reinforce course content. These are succinct, contained, and highly regimented tasks that students perform to underscore and practice what they've learned. There are a variety of forms of exercise I introduce. When students are learning method, we practice the method; when students are learning theory, we leverage exercises to further explore and build their perspectives on the content.

In both cases, exercises have these qualities or traits.

- **Exercises are "time boxed."** We set aside a specific amount of time for each activity, and I actively monitor that time. I set a timer and end the exercise promptly at that time. This means that students need to focus. Left without a time constraint, they will spin and spin. When they know they will have to share their work in a short period of time (10 or 15 minutes), their attention is sharpened.

- **Exercises have very detailed, very constraining parameters.** For example, if students are exploring how to create a customer journey map, I'll give them instructions like this:

    - Produce a customer journey map based on your research data.

    - Start by listing the stages a user will go through to accomplish their goals.

    - Map those stages to the journey map across the y axis.

    - The map should include 5 of these stages

    - Sketch swim lanes for "people", "processes", "emotions", and "artifacts."

    - Fill in the activities as black circles, highlighting problems as red squares.

    - The map should be sketched on a large piece of paper that is 2' by 3'.

You'll see that the constraints are very limiting. By dramatically containing what the students can do, the exercise purposefully focuses on the most important part—in this case, thinking about experience over time. The actual mechanics of the diagram are less important than the idea of time-based interactions.

Exercises are almost always conducted in a group. Groupwork in class helps reinforce ways to work through ideas together. Groupwork also serves the additional goal of including more introverted students, who feel more comfortable offering their opinions in a smaller and more intimate setting.

When students have completed the exercises, I'll often skip a formal share-out of the work, and instead focus on a reflection of the exercise itself. Skipping a share-out seems strange, and students often want to present what they've done to the group. But I've found that the raw nature of the things they've produced makes these artifacts nearly incomprehensible to other teams, and during a share-out, teams are distracted by thinking about their own work. They don't pay attention. Instead, I'll hold a group discussion. By focusing that introspection on a reflective conversation (a meta-conversation about the exercise itself), teams can speak more to the generalized process of making the artifacts and less about any individual artifact. Instead of saying *"Show us what you made"*, I'll ask students to *"Tell us how that felt."*

Visual exploration through diagramming

When students create visual representations of ideas, they create boundary conditions around complexity and ambiguity. By creating a diagram like a concept map—a map that connects ideas (often nouns and verbs) of a situation—they add shape to an idea. This shape can shift and change over time, but it creates a sense of pseudo-objectivity, which makes a problem tractable.

Diagrams can be created individually or collaboratively, and when they are created in teams, dialogue becomes the major force behind making decisions or diagrammatic "moves." Students talk through vague concepts, forge connections between ideas, and bring ideas into focus by saying "it is this, not that." I spark this form of diagramming in class explicitly: "OK, let's try to make sense of what we just discussed. In pairs, create a concept map or other form of diagram that captures and visualizes your knowledge of the content we've studied."

Role play

Role play is another form of exercise. During role play, students take on personas and then play out how those personas might react in a given situation. Role play is about imagining and about active empathy. When acting as another person, it forces students to see the world from their perspective: shifting the camera away from their own viewpoint, and hypothesizing what a different person might think.

It might look like this. A pair of students may take a particular reading that we've been discussing. One may take on the role of the author, and another may play the role of a practicing designer. And then the two can begin to have a conversation. The student who is playing the role of the author can leverage the content in the reading to make informed hypothesis about reaction, and the other student can provoke that form of reaction.

For example, if the students are exploring a paper about how designers should focus on usability instead of aesthetics, the role-play may look like this:

> Student 1, acting as a practicing designer: "I enjoyed hearing about your concepts, but I fundamentally disagree. My work is all about aesthetics; my clients hire me to make products that are beautiful."

> Student 2, acting as the author: "But beauty alone isn't enough. I described how objects of beauty are often purchased but left un-used; do you remember the example I gave about the beautiful, but useless, teapot?"

> Student 1: "Yes, but you missed something in the example—the person purchased that useless teapot. So the company that sold it made money on the sale."

> Student 2: "I don't believe that simply selling the teapot is enough. That's about corporatism, not about design. We have more of a re-sponsibility to make objects that people want to use, not just objects people want to buy."

In this short role-play, the students first start by discussing a point of view the author takes. But quickly, they introduce concepts that the author *didn't* say—they hypothesize about how the author may have felt about a hypothetical situation. This means that the student playing the author is thinking critically about the author's argument and applying it in a new context. There's a conflict between the two students—a new idea has emerged, and the conflict can be discussed and resolved.

This form of role play is important for several reasons. One is that it pushes a student to try to empathize with another person, a person with more experience. This means that they need to form connections between their own experiences and what they've read or learned about someone else's experience. They are literally playing a role, one student acting as a working professional (which they aren't) and another as an author (which they aren't).

Forced conflict and resolution

In-class exercises can also focus on conflict and resolution. I don't mean a behavioral conflict; instead, I mean a conflict of ideas, positioning someone's beliefs against someone else's. The classroom is a place where conflict can be managed, and through a form of meta-conversation, I can act to referee the conflict so that it's a conflict of perspectives, not a conflict of people. That is, it's not the people that are positioned in opposition—it's their ideas.

Conflict is valuable because it gives students an opportunity to examine an idea from another perspective. Their existing worldview is challenged, and I can help them explore *why* that view is being challenged. The intent of conflict is not to change one's mind. Instead, it's to explore alternative perspectives. In engaging in a conflict, a student must make a reasoned case or argument for their idea. This means that they need to anticipate opposition, think critically about the things they hear from other students, craft an argument for why their view is important, and leverage persuasion to attempt to convince others that their ideas are right.

Conflict doesn't work without a trusted moderator. The professor acts as that neutral party by stopping the conflict periodically to force a check-in. *Why are your views in opposition? What pieces of the argument are most salient and which are weakest?* For *this* to work, the professor needs to have the trust and respect of the students. Students need to see me as objective even when I'm making rhetorical comments that challenge an established view. This trust comes slowly, which means this technique works best later in a class.

CRITIQUE

Critique is a special type of learning experience that happens during a design studio. It emphasizes the negative in order to help students improve their work. During critique, students present their work to a group. The group identifies places where the work can improve. They discuss alternative solutions, sketch those solutions, and work collaboratively to explore which changes will benefit the work the most.

The pin up

A critique begins as a student displays and presents their work. I emphasize the physicality of design deliverables—I ask students to print out their work and pin it up on the wall. This is true even for digital items, like screens, presentations, or animations (for presentations, I have the students print their slides. For animations, I have the students print keyframes of their videos). When the work is displayed on the wall, several things happen.

First, the entire group can all observe the work at once. This means that they are all baselined on what the student has done, all responding to the same work, and all sharing an understanding of the scope and breadth of creative material.

Next, the group can see the work in an end-to-end story. Design always exists in a narrative context, and seeing the work on the wall gives physical expanse so that each student can read the story. This is often a series of frames; for example, if the student is presenting the redesign of a mobile application, they can show each frame in sequence. This means that the group can respond not only to the interface on any given screen, but also to the flow a user will experience through the product—it helps ground the critique in both detail but also in behavior.

Additionally, pinning up the work physically instead of displaying it on a screen helps the student learn the best ways to communicate complex ideas to an audience (a skill they will need constantly when they are working professionally). The first time a student pins up, they inevitably realize that the work is too small, too light, lacking annotation, and often nearly incomprehensible to the other students. This gives us an opportunity to discuss presentation and persuasion, and how every form of presentation (including critique) is an opportunity to shape opinion and comprehension.

The critique

Once the work is pinned up, the critique begins. While it's tempting for the student to explain the work, I encourage them to only describe the "rules of engagement", and then simply step back and let the group begin. The work should be self-explanatory. An explanation seems harmless, but it actually presents a defensive position, as if the student needs to rationalize their design decisions. That creates a dynamic of "me vs. them", and that's not healthy in a critique.

Instead, I teach students to describe the *parameters* of the critique. This might be a description of the type of feedback they are looking for, or the actual mechanics they want for the critique. For example, they may say:

"For this critique, I want to focus on the way I've laid out the navigation for the user. I would like feedback on if the navigation is clear. Please don't offer feedback on the graph down here, because I'm still working on that."

This sets up boundaries for the critique, and says that some things are off limits.

After they establish the rules of critique, I ask the student to be quiet. Depending on how advanced the class is, I either take a backseat myself, or I start the critique. Early in a student's educational journey, they are afraid to speak their mind. In these cases, I'll start the critique by pointing out an element that isn't working, and I'll offer suggestions on how to improve it. The benefit of starting the critique is that students see and can emulate the way I phrase my comments. There's a challenge, though; younger or less experienced students will often follow my lead—they will agree with what I say and be afraid to voice a dissenting opinion.

No matter if I start the critique or someone else begins, I exemplify the behavior I want students to have—I sketch directly on top of the student's work with design changes and suggestions. When a student offers criticism, I'll prompt them to "show us" instead of telling us. Drawing a solution has several benefits. It captures the idea so that the designer has a record of it later. And, it forces a level of specificity from the critiquer; they can't simply say things like "that isn't working" because they have to propose a way to make it work.

During the critique, I pay attention to, and correct, language from the students. When they say things like "I don't like that" or "That's weird", I prompt them—"what do you mean?" I ask them to focus on problems, not positive elements or things that are working. I ask them to explain why they react in a certain way. What about the design is bad? What prompted the comment that something is "weird"?

Sometimes, a critique feels like it's turning personal. I'll see the person who has the work on the wall becoming defensive and starting to entrench—defending their work, and ignoring the benefits of the critique. When this happens, I'll stop the critique and hold a meta conversation. Instead of critiquing the work, we'll critique the critique itself. I'll point out how the person became defensive, and we'll brainstorm ways to avoid this type of reaction in the future.

As the critique continues, I'll constantly remind students of the rules of engagement and best practices. These typically include prompts to offer suggestions for improvement, to sketch solutions, and to identify problems and not just good qualities.

After the critique

When a critique is over, I'll often ask the student if they are aware of what they will change in future iterations. This causes a level of summative reflection—it encourages them to replay the critique, quickly, and make sure they synthesized the content with enough detail that they can move forward.

Less experienced students will have lost a lot of the detail of the critique. They will feel overwhelmed with the amount of feedback they received, and sometimes they will leave the critique feeling less directed than when it started. I anticipate this during the critique when I don't see students capturing or writing down the conversation. Again, I'll hold a critique about the critique—I'll stop the critique and say "I noticed you weren't writing this down. You probably won't be able to remember this all later. As the critique goes on, there are a few ways you can handle this. You can write down ideas yourself, or you can assign one of your classmates to be the scribe. This way, you'll be able to get more value out of this conversation."

Frequency

Early in their studies, there's a mental hurdle for students to work through. A student, assigned a project, works as hard as they could on it. The project is difficult for them, and it takes a long time. When they are confronted with negative criticism, they feel like their effort was wasted, and further steps seem insurmountable. They say to themselves, "There's no way I can make something like this again."

To get around this, I hold critique as frequently as possible. I don't wait for a student to be "done" with a project before encouraging criticism of it. In this way, the goal of an in-class critique isn't just to improve the work. It's also to instill a culture of criticism for the student so they stop seeing their work as precious. Design is iterative and is never done, and if a student starts to treat their work as "finished", they will be reluctant to change it even when confronted with a better solution. A culture of criticism means that critique becomes just another part of the design process, just like research, sketching, or user testing.

PRESENTATION

Students in my courses constantly present their work. In an 8 week quarter, they may present as frequently as four times each week; in our 32 week curriculum, that's as many as 120 presentations. I emphasize presentation for a variety of reasons.

First, a presentation suggests that work that is incomplete can always be shared. Design work doesn't require a dramatic "unveiling" of a finished product. In my professional work, I've observed that this sort of monumental presentation of "finished work" nearly always falls flat. Stakeholders don't want to be surprised. They want to be brought along through the process.

Additionally, by constantly presenting design work, students build a vocabulary for talking about complex and ambiguous problems and solutions. They become conversant in describing ideas so that an audience can understand them. Non-designers often don't know how to respond to design work—they may say "I like it" or "I don't like it." Stakeholders want to understand design work, but they don't always have the working vocabulary or internal mental model of creativity to appropriately understand it. They are often looking for someone to help guide them through the work so that they can shape a more refined per-spective on it. As students gain a vocabulary for design, they can help an audience better articulate their response so the work can be further improved.

Constant presentation also helps students gain confidence about their abilities. They slowly overcome the idea that their work isn't worthy of attention, because they constantly have to call attention to it. Students work through shame to arrive at strength.

There are different types of presentations. Students may give a formal presentation, with people sitting in rows watching them orate from the front of the room. It can also be ad-hoc, as someone wanders by, or online through a conference call. But in all cases, the student needs to be prepared to tell a compelling story—to weave a "narrative arc" around the work in a way that makes sense. This means setting the context for the work, thinking about the best format in which to share work, avoiding assumptions about what an audience knows, and then leveraging strong presentation skills to deliver their content effectively.

Setting context

During the first presentation a student gives, they typically fail to set the context for their work. This means that they don't describe what the assignment was, what their intention was in solving the problem, and what the constraints were. Often, they fail to describe what they did and why they did it, and instead simply show the work. This seems more "honest" to them; they feel that the work should stand on its own.

But design work needs a background narrative to it. Students need to help an audience understand the parameters in which the work was crafted. This means sharing even simple things: what's the intention of the presentation? Is it to share final design work as a form of celebration? Is it to show in-progress work, and ask for criticism and feedback?

Is it to share the whole body of work, or to simply focus on an individual component? Without instruction, an audience will judge what's put in front of them through whatever lens they happen to have. Students need to set the context for feedback.

After a student presents (typically for the first time), I'll offer a very pointed critique of their presentation style, not of presentation content. It may look like this:

During your presentation, you jumped directly into the content. You didn't share who you were, what the purpose of the presentation was, what sort of criticism you wanted, and what you hoped to gain from the presentation. Without telling these things to the audience, they won't understand how to frame and consider your work. They'll be left on their own to interpret the context of the work, and that means that you'll receive a mess of feedback. It won't be focused, and so it won't be actionable. On future presentations, make sure you are explicit in setting the boundaries of a presentation. Tell the audience who you are and where you are in the design process. Be clear about what they will see, and why they are seeing it. And make sure to tell them what you hope to learn. Set the limits to critique, describing what is in bounds and what is out of bounds.

This form of direct presentation criticism helps the student begin to take control of their presentations. They realize that a presentation needs to be treated just like any other design problem; it's about presenting the content through a persuasive narrative. My feedback gives them ways to improve, such as setting the boundaries and context of the presentation.

Presentation methods & skills

Students typically gravitate towards a Powerpoint or Keynote presentation because they've constantly seen other people use these tools. But there are other formats that may be more effective for presenting work. For example, one very effective way to present in-flight design work is to "walk the wall"—gathering audience participants around a working war-room wall and telling both a process and content story. This describes not only what the student did, but also why they did it. Showing sketches, rather than polished slides, helps an audience feel like the work is a draft, and that means they will be more willing to offer their own suggestions on changes. They don't feel as though the work is completed, and so they don't feel as though their recommendations will be ignored.

Another form of effective presentation is to use a printed out document as the main set of content. A simple one or two page handout can be used to indicate to a group that the goal is to have an informal discussion, rather than look at finished work. This typically says "let's start with this content, but I'm open to the conversation moving around." In this context, the student may be best served using a whiteboard to capture content as it's discussed. I help students understand that when they control the whiteboard, they control the room. What they write down becomes the frame for conversation, and this is powerful. A simple handout can spark the conversation, and then the whiteboard can be used to guide that conversation.

I teach students raw presentation skills, because I've found that they have no idea what to do when faced with the prospect of standing up in front of other people and sharing ideas. I teach both the concepts of a presentation but also the detailed, tactical mechanics of delivering content.

First, I instruct students that every presentation is a chance for them to gain something or lose something. If they present effectively, they've gained buy-in or credibility. An audience will leave with a positive view not only of their content but also of them. That's important in a professional context because ideas live or die based on how people feel, not necessarily based on objective criteria and assessment. If a presentation goes poorly, they've lost an opportunity to gain something, such as funding, credibility, acknowledgement, or helpful criticism. Learning that every presentation is positive or negative helps students gain an understanding of the value of the presentation itself, and to treat it as equally as important as their design work itself.

Students also learn that every presentation is a structured conversation, even if they are the only one talking. In a conversation, you don't just jump into your main point; you work to understand the viewpoint of the people you are talking to, and your ideas intertwine with theirs. A conversation is empathetic, as you try to see what the other person sees and feel what they feel. The dynamics of a conversation are often around sharing an idea or a story. Presentations are the same. As students start to think about a presentation as a conversation, they more actively consider what the audience knows or doesn't know. They become more aware of their audience.

Typically, when students are starting out, they make poor assumptions about their audience. They forget that the audience probably doesn't know anything at all about their work. This is particularly true when guests are invited to class. Students will jump right into their content, and the audience will remain puzzled through much of the presentation. Because they don't know what the student was trying to achieve, they don't know the limits or constraints that the student worked with during their exploration. And this means that the students will receive all sorts of feedback, most of which is not relevant or actionable. When this happens, the Q&A portion of the presentation inevitably goes sideways, as audience members hone in on details that are less important or less relevant.

For example, a student may have locked down the overall concept design and be looking for detailed feedback on things like font choice or composition. But if they don't articulate that to the audience, everything is fair game. The audience will probably critique the overall idea, and that isn't useful to the student; they've wasted an opportunity for valuable feedback.

I also teach students that a presentation requires them to feed the energy in the room, and their participants consume that energy. They should leave a presentation feeling proud but exhausted, because it means they've put the force of their personality into it. A presentation is often a show, and that means that the audience needs to both understand the content but also feel positive about the decisions they've made or ideas they've learned. This is reinforced by the presenter's demeanor. If the student talks slowly and in a monotone, the audience will lose interest and stop being engaged. But if the student is clearly excited about the content, that enthusiasm is contagious.

Part of engaging with an audience is "reading the room." This is about observing how participants are reacting (are they yawning? are they playing with their phones?) and adjusting both content and style accordingly. In a small group presentation, if people aren't paying attention, the presenter can gently call this out and can shift the presentation agenda accordingly: "I think maybe this content isn't resonating as much as I hoped it would. Are there other things we could cover instead that would be a better use of time?" Often, this is enough to bring the room back into focused attention.

When students are just learning how to present, they typically end with "Well, that's about it." This is probably the worst way to end a presentation. It leaves the audience feeling a sense of doubt instead of a sense of confidence. Additionally, it leaves the room open to a chaotic question and answer session.

I teach students to end with a more confident summary of what they've presented, and to set the stage for the types of questions they would like to address. For example, if they've been presenting a new way of thinking about a business strategy, I'll instruct them to end their presentation by saying, "Today, we've discussed the new business strategy I'm proposing. We covered why I think it's important, and the actionable way we'll implement it. At this point, I would like to take questions. Specifically, I would like to hear about implementability. Do you feel that this work can be easily implemented?"

This type of ending is valuable for a few reasons. First, it summarizes the content—it helps the audience remember why they are there, and what they should take away from the presentation. It opens the room to questions, but only to questions of a certain type. And it steers the conversation to start with a specific area (can the work be easily implemented?) instead of leaving it open ended.

Q&A

There's an art to fielding questions from the audience. I teach students to anticipate several types of common questions.

First, a question may be purposefully antagonistic. Working professionals frequently find themselves presenting contentious material to politically charged audiences. Strategic design content may challenge someone's authority or agenda. So, we practice responding to overtly mean criticism. I'll role-play an offensive and rude audience member, asking them impossible questions and making statements like "This doesn't make any sense" or "There's no way we can do this", or even "That's a terrible, stupid idea." I'll warn students ahead of time that questions like this may be coming, but I'll also surprise them. And, when the presentation is over, we always hold a reflection session so the student can describe how they felt and we can critique their response to the question.

There's another form of question that's common—the non-question. Audience members will offer a monologue, never actually arriving at a question. Students don't know how to respond to this form of interaction, so we practice responding to a comment with further discussion instead of an awkward silence. This may be to build on the comment, or to redirect the comment towards the student's agenda. This reinforces that the student, as presenter, is in control of the presentation experience, but that they need to bring the audience along for the ride.

Sometimes, questions are just not good. Questioners ask about things that don't make sense, or content that's already been covered. Students learn to respond positively in these cases, to build credibility, rather than cutting down the questioner. Instead of ignoring the question or shutting it down, they may say something like "That's a great question", and then steer the conversation in a positive direction.

Getting prepared

In addition to ending a presentation effectively, students need to understand how to start—how to prepare even before the audience arrives.

First, we discuss setting up the physical space. This includes simple things like removing clutter, organizing the chairs, wiping down tables, and even sweeping the floor. Everything impacts how someone will view and consider a presentation, and most students won't think about things like this because they are so concerned with the presentation itself. They need to understand the importance of presenting a professional demeanor, even with the workspace.

I also teach students to become aware of their technology. They need to test their laptops with the projector to make sure it works. They need to understand how basic things, like the sound system in the room, work. I reinforce that these things matter: if they don't understand how the technology works, the audience will lose faith in their ability to design with technology. It's subtle, but lack of skill in one area can impact perception of skill in another area. Something as simple as trying a laptop ahead of time means they will be prepared to set up quickly and effectively during the actual presentation.

We spend a lot of time talking about emergencies and contingencies. What happens if the projector breaks? What happens if the laptop breaks? Once, I was presenting to a large audience of over 500 people and my laptop decided to reboot itself. I had a choice—I could stand around and awkwardly wait for it to finish, or I could keep presenting. I kept on going. It's not fair to the ideas or to the audience to simply wait, and I would feel terrible. We practice what to do when that sort of thing happens. During presentations, I'll sometimes pull the plug on the students halfway through. They need to learn how to proceed with confidence. This prompts a productive group conversation around ways to handle a technical meltdown.

I instruct students to carry backups of their presentation content on a USB stick, on the internet, and on their phone. If they are unable to present from their laptop, they can always present from someone else's. If they have the presentation on their phone and their laptop breaks, they can use the small slides on their phone's screen as speaking notes for themselves so they can continue presenting. Our mantra is to "always have a backup."

We also discuss the details of the slides themselves. First, I teach students that the presentation is for them, not for the audience. This seems counterintuitive—aren't the slides there so the audience can follow along? In fact, I treat the slides as a signpost for myself so that I know what I want to say and when I want to say it. I can glance at the slide and instantly recall where I am in the overall narrative of the presentation.

This means that each slide has less on it, often just a single word, quote, or picture, and that I know my content cold. It *doesn't* mean that I've memorized the content, and that's a hurdle students have to get over. Many have learned (in high school, typically) that practice means memorization, and this is something I need to have them unlearn because a memorized presentation feels forced. And, if there's some sort of interaction during the middle of a presentation, such as a question from the audience, students who memorize will be thrown off track.

One of the biggest hurdles students need to overcome is reading their own slides. When students first present, they include a lot of text on a single slide, and they then read exactly what they've written. When they do this the first time, I stop them in the middle and immediately correct that behavior. I explain to them that reading the slide is rude to the audience. The audience can read it on their own. And, it's boring to watch. It's not engaging. Then, I have the student start again from the beginning. This is a hard problem for students to overcome, and I may need to repeat this for several students over the course of the quarter.

Students learn that subtle details on the slides matter. This means simple things, like having pixel-perfect alignment of images, spell checking, and using a consistent font and color scheme. These details add up, and when they are ignored, it can feel like "death by a thousand papercuts." One of the ways students learn this is by printing out their presentation and critiquing it, just like any other deliverable. We can draw directly on the presentation, circle things that can be improved, and students can iterate on the presentation itself in addition to the content.

Students need to learn not only how to structure a presentation, but also how to literally hold themselves during the presentation. We discuss things like posture and body positions. Where do you put your hands? (Not in your pockets or on your hips) Where do you make eye contact? (With everyone, slowly) Do you sit or stand? Do you walk around the room, or stay planted in one place? These are just like other skills. Students need to learn these things, because no one has ever told them before. To practice and analyze these things, I film the students and then we watch the recording. We analyze and critique the student's presentation dynamics, focusing not on the content, but on how they present themselves to the audience.

THEORY AND DIALOGUE

Some of my classes are rich with theory. Students take theory classes that focus on the social and political relationships between design and the culture of society. They learn to think about designing for the public sector, specifically as it relates to ill-defined problem solving and the ethical obligations of designers. They read complex articles from computer scientists, psychologists, and sociologists, and they build arguments that synthesize these articles into new ideas.

Yet my classes are focused on practitioners, and these students go on to be practicing designers, not academics. They work for big brands, for consultancies, and in startups—and increasingly, they start their own entrepreneurial endeavors. They aren't pursuing a Ph.D., so why teach theory? Why waste precious class time on academic discourse, rather than practical skills?

I've thought a lot about what makes a whole designer. One of the qualities is craft and immediacy with material. That's sort of obvious—someone who makes things needs to be good at making things.

But if they only make things and never question the things they make, they are simply a hired set of hands. I'm convinced that theory is also a key ingredient to greatness, a key part of claiming to be a competent, professional designer. There are at least three reasons I think students need to learn theory as part of their foundational design education.

Theory gives students the basis for an opinion about their process.
A huge amount of design work is subjective. Design research—applied ethnography—gives designers the basis to form a *specific* opinion in the context of a design problem; it's deliberate and is often used to substantiate a design decision. But theory gives a designer the basis to have an informed governing philosophy for the *process they'll use to do their work*.

For example, design research might indicate that homeless people in Texas have different shelter requirements than homeless people in Detroit. It can offer specific details about those contexts and people, and can then be used to substantiate design decisions. *Theory* about the ethics of designing with at-risk populations can inform the process used to work with those populations. How do you engage with a population that can't give informed consent? What does it mean to drive a participatory design process, as compared with a top-down process? What steps should a designer take to translate their findings into actionable insights? Theory holds the answers to these process questions, and for a student of design, it presents an evolving body of knowledge that they can lean on as they develop their own methodology for engaging with large-scale problems.

Theory gives students the ability to think beyond a single design problem, in order to develop higher-order organizing principles. Each design problem is unique. But after encountering a number of design problems, designers start to realize that there are patterns to both problems and solutions. Identifying these patterns takes time and comes with experience. Theory gives a designer a structure in which to organize their experiences—a way of thinking about the sameness and differentness. It becomes an intellectual taxonomy and a way of organizing different types of design patterns.

After years of working as a consultant, I've built up a portfolio of work in fields like telecom, consumer goods, entertainment, enterprise software, and so on. That's not a very useful way to categorize my work, though, because it doesn't give me a way to draw insight from the work and apply it on future projects. Instead, I try to think about how my work relates to theoretical constructs. Some of my work is related to complex problem solving and explores ill-structured and well-structured problems. Some of my work is related to experience and engagement, and leans heavily on ideas related to affect and learning theory. By reflecting on my work as it relates to larger abstract ideas, I can better think across design problems, and better apply knowledge from one professional experience to another.

Theory gives students a sense of purpose, a reason for doing their work. Theory holds a larger meaning for design work, as it grounds it in a cultural context of human want and need. As we reflect on the hours we spend at a job, design theory provides a reason for our hard work, a reason other than "just a paycheck." We work in design because design changes the world, humanizes technology, and improves the quality of the human experience. Reading and discussing design discourse helps students remember that.

We're seeing an influx of design programs aimed at practitioners, programs that intend to increase the number of designers available to work in the increasingly complex technological landscape. I'm skeptical of programs that don't include theory, dialogue, and debate in their curriculum. It has been argued that vocational programs should focus on core skills and ignore the larger academic, theoretical subject matter. I would argue the opposite. It is the vocational programs that require this thoughtful context the most, as graduates from these programs will have a direct impact on the products and services that shape our world.

To teach theory, I curate a set of readings around various themes. These themes are things like "Power", "Manipulation", or "Social Impact"— big, complex and gnarly topics. I try to pick readings that present unique and often conflicting viewpoints, with authors that back up their viewpoints with case studies and examples. The readings are a mix of popular writing (newspaper or blog articles), and academic writing (formal journal articles).

In class, we discuss the readings. I provoke debate and conversation using a Socratic style. I ask open-ended questions, juxtaposing one viewpoint against another. I urge students to expand on their thoughts, structure their comments in a meaningful way, and start to develop a unique and synthesized perspective on the readings (instead of simply summarizing what the author said).

When we have these conversations, our focus is on exploration. As a facilitator of the discussion, my role is to ask open ended questions and then encourage all students to actively participate. These questions may take the form of "What do you think the author meant here?" or "Can you think of a time where you encountered this principle in your own life or work?"

These verbal prompts, and the subsequent discussion, are analysis prompts. We examine the structure of the paper and the author's argument. Through this examination, we identify what the author said, and try to interpret what the author meant. This interpretation is the first form of synthesis—of making meaning out of data. But synthesis is difficult in a group setting, where comments and ideas fly fast and loose. Some students process the information by talking through it aloud, while others reflect quietly.

It's my responsibility to be aware of which students are external processors and which are more introspective. A professor friend once told me that the look on the face of a student thinking very hard, and on the face of a student who is bored to tears, is the same. He's right; I can't just judge the looks students have on their faces. Instead, I need to form a more intimate connection with my students so I know their particular learning style, and there's no shortcuts for this—it just takes time and effort. So, a fundamental part of teaching and learning theory is having a personalized, individualized relationship with the professor.

LECTURE

You'll notice that a "lecture" format is missing from my list of in-class teaching methods I use. I try very, very hard to stay away from a pure lecture format. There's a place for lecture, focused on knowledge dissemination; this is effective when the professor knows facts and content and needs the class to know them too. But this is perhaps the least experiential form of learning, and the least effective.

It's tempting to resort to a lecture because it's controllable. There are less variables, less things left to the dynamic of the classroom. But that is also why the method is ineffective. A lecture doesn't give room for change or adaptation. It says to the students, "you are less important than the professor", which, in a creative field, is simply not true. It's rare that the professor has the right answer because design solutions are not right or wrong, but only better or worse. The student, their work, and their ideas serve to complete the dialogue.

When I do need to communicate information in a top-down autocratic fashion, I keep these session as short as possible, often less than 15 minutes. And, these sessions are framed with interactive and experiential learning to ensure that they have relevance—that they are contextualized in a broader view of the subject matter.

Assignments

Creative learning requires practice, and while practice is done in a studio environment under the helpful eye of the professor, a lot of the experience of learning comes through individual and group assignments—work that's done without the professor there to act as a guide or facilitator. In these cases, students need to think critically to transform often vague or conflicting assignment criteria into actionable constraints, and then work to solve a given problem. Homework isn't just about learning skills. It's also about learning to be self-sufficient.

There are several common types of assignments that I use. These include iterating on a design, practicing a method, building craft, and developing a perspective on new ideas.

ITERATING ON A DESIGN

I frequently assign students a project focused on rapid iteration. In this type of assignment, a student creates something (a presentation, a series of wireframes, a service blueprint) and then iterates on that artifact over, and over, and over. For example, in a class focused on digital product design, I assign students the task of creating a redesign for an existing digital product, such as a banking application. I'll instruct them to:

Using the existing banking application:

- Identify ten problems in the current design.

- Redesign the application to fix those problems

- User test your redesign with at least 10 people

- Hold a group critique with your classmates

- Repeat this process.

In the first iteration, students inevitably produce an ugly, ill-structured, confusing redesign. I then have them user test this iteration with real people. We combine the result of user testing with an in-class critique, and then students highlight main areas of improvement. Then, their next task is to work through the problem again, refining what they've made; and then, to user test again, and so-on. In an 8 week quarter, we work through 7 iterations, each following the same model: make, test & critique, refine.

Each stage in the process comes with its own challenges.

Create a new design

When the student makes the first few iterations of their design, they encounter two main problems. The first is that the problem itself—such as redesigning a banking application—is hard. The problems they have been assigned are things that working professionals really work on;

they are advanced problem. Students aren't yet prepared to do a good job, and that means that their early iterations will be poor. They will make bad design decisions, creating products that are hard to use or overly complicated. This is discouraging for students because they can see that the results are poor—their taste is stronger than their design abilities.

The second problem students encounter is that the actual fidelity of their design is poor, too. It doesn't look the way they want, making it hard for someone else (like a user, or their classmates) to understand their intention. This means that, when people see the design, they can't comprehend what's happening at a tactical execution level—they won't understand that a button is supposed to be clickable, or that a draggable slider can be dragged, or that lorum-ipsem style text is actually instructional, and so-on. This is equally frustrating to the student because they know their own intent and have failed to communicate it to another person.

Test the design and hold a critique

The student is aware of both of these problems—that their work product is confusing, and that the execution of the work product is impacting comprehension. But they usually only know that these problems exist at a general level. They know there is a problem, but they haven't yet learned to pinpoint what the problems are.

This is clarified through user testing. Students leverage the think aloud style I've already discussed: they present their work to people (I instruct them to test with people they've never met before, not their friends or classmates), and ask them to use their rough sketched prototypes to accomplish specific goals. For example, when redesigning the banking application, a user may be prompted to *"Use these wireframes to deposit a check, and talk out loud as you accomplish the task."* Students capture what the user says, but they don't intervene to help—they let the user continue on the task even when they run into problems or can't understand what to do next.

This form of testing is critical to moving a design forward, as it produces further constraints for future iterations and highlights areas that need improvement. Testing helps students see that what they made is confusing, and most importantly, it highlights that confusion in specifics. It's not that the interface as a whole is *generally* confusing—it's that this particular button is hard to see, or this specific text is full of jargon, or this navigation element is hard to understand. The specificity is actionable because a student now knows what to fix. The problem feel more manageable. Instead of struggling in the face of "fixing the whole design", the student can hone in on specific changes to make (to a button, or text, or a navigation element).

Testing also reinforces to the student that their work is always malleable and that there isn't a "done" state for design work. Usability testing will always highlight problems, and testing each iteration produces actionable redesign recommendations. Students slowly begin to realize that the goal of design is not to "solve the problem all at once" but to "improve their work over time."

In addition to testing with users, students also test with their classmates through the methods of structured critique that we've already discussed.

They pin their work on the wall, step back, and the class tries to understand what they did and why they did it. Through the critique, students identify problems, articulate solutions, and most importantly, sketch those solutions directly on each other's work.

Refine the design

The output of user testing and critique is detailed and actionable. These methods give the student a sense for what they need to change in future iterations. After testing and critique, students synthesize the findings from these methods in order to produce another iteration.

This challenges them to identify the most important feedback and to make sense of it. Feedback is often ill-structured and incomplete, and they need to translate it into something actionable. They need to be selective and establish their own criteria for what to redesign—they need to prioritize only the feedback that they see as productive, and turn those comments and suggestions into changes.

Students work through seven full iterations (create, test & critique, refine), producing a new iteration each week. This fast cadence helps to instill and reinforce several key behaviors.

- **Students learn to work quickly**. They can't labor over a single design, because there's simply no time. The schedule doesn't let them second guess their own decisions. They need to make decisions without "all of the data" and move forward, leveraging external feedback as the primary vehicle to help them assess their decisions.

- **Students realize that iteration always leads to improvement**. The act of making something is not simply to communicate it to someone else. It's actually a form of learning. Each iteration changes what the designer knows, and they become smarter about the design as they make it. More iterations lead to more knowledge production.

- **Students learn the value of critique and user testing in providing new provocation for design**. They learn to ask for critique, rather than avoid it, because they see how external input helps them look at old problems in new ways. Usability testing reinforces that "the user is not like me" and helps them make their solutions more usable and useful.

- **Students build confidence**. Students start out ashamed of what they make, because it doesn't make sense, doesn't look like how they want it to look, and feels incomplete and sloppy. Over the duration of the course, this changes. Their artifacts look more realistic, and they better capture intent: they seem more cohesive and more professional. Students feel more competent, and feel more confident in their decisions.

PRACTICING A METHOD

An iteration assignment helps students learn to work quickly and ideate through a problem. Another type of assignment I use focuses on practicing a method. A method is a discrete set of tasks or steps that can be used to achieve a goal; this might be a method like we've already discussed, such as Heuristic Evaluation (which identifies usability problems in a product), Journey Mapping (which helps describe how people interact with a system over time), or sketching in perspective (drawing shapes that look realistic, in "3d"). In each case, students learn how to do the method in class, and are then assigned to do the same method out of class.

When I teach methods, and reinforce them through assignments, I emphasize really specific steps—I tell the student exactly what to do. I've found that if I ask students to "create a customer journey map" after they've learned the method, they struggle. Even though they've heard about the method in class, and even if they've practiced it several times in class, they don't know what to do or what order in which to do it when they are on their own. But if I assign them the exact steps ("First, create a timeline by drawing a horizontal line on a large piece of paper. Next, label the individual stages that a user goes through as they experience the product. Next..."), they flourish.

In the context of learning methods, this level of explicit solutioning helps them build "muscle memory" for the method. When they first encounter a new way to do something, they will probably do it wrong. By providing the explicit steps, students find that they can do the hardest part—start. Starting provides an artifact that they can respond to. And then, like other assignment types, they can iterate. They can do the process again, this time working without the explicit steps. Iteration one is mandated top-down; further iterations are worked bottom up.

DEVELOPING CRAFT

Another form of assignment I use is intended to develop craftsmanship.

Meet someone who has completed four years of design education and ask them to reflect on their education, and they'll likely tell you stories of the dreaded foundations assignments. These craft oriented projects focus narrowly on a single "core" of design, like color, or line, or texture, or shadow. I remember some of these projects from my color theory class. We were to select a magazine layout, pin it to a board, and examine it. And then, our task was to recreate the layout, exactly, using tiny 1/8" square pieces of colored paper. It took forever (my memory of freshman year is a bit tired, but I recall it taking close to 100 hours), and at the time, we all questioned the point. What on earth could we learn from such a menial and monotonous activity, and how was this a good use of our really expensive education?

In fact, the foundational year of design education is full of activities like this. Paint a hundred color blocks a single color, but with a complete spectrum of saturation. Draw every letter of a single typeface, as realistically as possible. Sand a perfect sphere out of a cube. Sand a hundred perfect spheres out of a hundred cubes.

In a word, these projects were intended to teach *craftsmanship*, and many have historic roots in Bauhaus education, or pre-Bauhaus arts and crafts approaches to the production of artifacts. By focusing on a simple, contained, and tedious task, students form tacit skills necessary for visual communication. Specifically, these projects offer some specific benefits to students.

First, Craft-oriented design projects help develop "muscle memory" related to visual acuity and fine motor skills. By performing a task over and over, we can focus attention and increase speed, precision, and the "automatic" quality of an action. A sense of fluidity and ease is developed during the process, and students gain confidence in taking visual action without introspection.

Additionally, craft-oriented design projects force students to "look closer", and encourage them to consider the details. Details are individually small and insignificant, but in aggregate, detailed design decisions contribute to a sense of thoroughness, completion, professionalism, and refinement. Students learn what a material can and cannot do, and are able to see how they can both respect and control a given material at a detailed level of precision.

The craft of strategy, interaction design, and entrepreneurship is not the same as the craft of more traditional design disciplines, like graphic design or industrial design. We already discussed foundational skills like contextual research, synthesis, service design, usability evaluation and product management. Craftsmanship in these contexts is in inference.

Craft through inference

We don't typically think of an inference (a leap in logic) as something that requires craftsmanship. But this is one of the fundamental skills of strategic design work, and it's something that can be practiced and refined over time. Inferences are important to the design process because, to create something new, we need to leverage incomplete (and often conflicting) data.

When they are first instructed to make inferences, students struggle. They've been trained, often from early stages of grade school, that making leaps in logic is a bad way to think about the world. It's sloppy science, and most of our education is rooted in a scientific, logical, rational approach.

The positivist way of thinking that they've learned is appropriate for learning science and trying to understand and explain natural phenomenon. But it doesn't make sense in a creative field, where our goal is to make new things.

Our profession is not a science, and we aren't trying to prove theories and hypotheses. Instead, we're often trying to provoke creativity. This provocation comes through the process of synthesis we already described: combining ideas in new and unexpected ways, developing insights from research data, identifying places where behavior can change, and creating simple visual models and diagrams of complex ideas.

When instructed to make inferences, students push back and demand more data. They constantly feel that, no matter how much research they have conducted, they don't have enough to prove that the ideas they develop are good ones. They are scared. How can they be sure that their designs will work?

Simply, they can't be sure. They can minimize risk through testing and iteration, but the success of an innovative new product, system or service is unknown because of its newness.

Craftsmanship here means making "good inferences." They don't always have to be believable, but students need to become comfortable "dialing up or down" the inference to match their intended level of innovation risk. Plausible leaps lead to less risky, but less exciting, new ideas. Larger leaps are less believable but drive towards more disruptive concepts. Understanding how to think about the impact of a leap on creativity is fundamental to establishing craft in inference. And, like any other craft-based skill, this requires constant practice.

We practice this skill each time a student goes through an ideation or prototyping cycle. I constantly push them to make their ideas more and more far-fetched, and to leap away from the gathered data and towards the realm of the unbelievable. And then, we discuss how to pull these ideas back. They sketch the crazy, but they also sketch the more believable. We compare their ideas to the research data. Can they track a direct line from the data to the idea? That's a tame idea. Tame doesn't mean bad. Often, successful innovations are incremental, and slight inferences are more appropriate.

This leads to a conversation of context. We review and consider the social and behavioral context for their work, to discuss the appropriateness of new ideas. For example, in the context of a new government service, students may have conducted research with government employees and citizens, and as they synthesized that data, they developed a series of insights about the behavior they observed. Some of the insights are believable, because they map one-to-one with the user data they observed. Some insights can be more readily challenged, as they make larger inferential leaps from the data. And some insights are outright unbelievable.

I can help students realize that government is typically a staid and conservative environment. If the level of inference is directly tied to the level of disruptive innovation, this is not a context that benefits from larger leaps—these will likely be met with skepticism, and their new products and services will be less successful.

Students need to explore different contexts to juxtapose different levels of speculation. This means that we assign a number of different styles of project, including civic engagement/government work, consulting-style visioning projects, and more traditional corporate work. This helps students practice craft through inference. Over time, and through this practice, they become more and more fluid and comfortable with this skill. They become more crisp in their inferences, just as they would become more and more detailed in sketching through repetitive practice.

Grading & Assessment

We've already discussed critique, a unique part of the design studio. Critique is a generative exercise, as it helps improve a design as the design comes to life. It happens continually through the design process.

But while critique is generative, students also benefit from hearing an evaluative form of criticism, something that's intended to help *them* improve, not just help their design improve. It's a subtle difference. Critique advances an idea, adding shape and definition to it. Evaluation helps a student reflect on the progress of their skill development and critical thinking abilities.

Students tend to continully self-assess based on the "quality of the thing they made" and the "quality of the things other people made." They look at their friends and the other people in their class, compare their work, and then judge themselves.

This form of comparative assessment can be useful, because it provides students with examples that they can build on. When they see how other students solved a problem, it can change their own perspective on the problem and offer new solutions. They can explore new pathways and approaches.

But comparative assessment is also harmful, because it reinforces to some students that their expectations are high and their skills are low. It can be demoralizing. What's more, it doesn't provide them with specific actions to take to improve—it simple says "your work is not as good as her work."

I've seen students react in two different ways when they focus on peer comparison. The first is that they give up. They feel that the divide between what they want to accomplish and what they *are* accomplishing is so great that it's insurmountable. They don't see a path from their own current skillset to the skills they need to succeed. And so they stop trying. They may literally give up, and drop out of the course or program. Or, they may figuratively stop trying, in the sense that they stop paying attention and stop putting effort into their learning. Both are destructive; both are hard to come back from.

The other way students react when peer comparison doesn't live up to their expectations is that they double-down on the thing they made and fight for it. They argue, and defend their abilities, and stop being open and receptive to evaluation of their skills. This is, in many ways, worse than giving up entirely. A combative response is a wall, something that makes learning impossible. And once it's there, that wall is really, really hard to tear down. It means that evaluation isn't being received, and self-reflection stops.

What's even more problematic is that the defensive feeling is like a virus. It infects the class, who then feel animosity towards that student. That's not fair to any of the students in the class, and can divide a growing sense of community in the group.

Since peer comparison can be harmful, it's important to introduce a variety of personal feedback, frequently, so students are guided towards a more productive style of introspection.

AN EXAMPLE ASSESSMENT

To understand how I deliver feedback, consider an example of a grade that I delivered to a student. This criticism was delivered in writing, but it's nearly identical to how I would deliver it in person. The student was working on a new product design, and had just finished writing a scenario about how a new user would use the product and presenting that scenario in class. This was a formal grading opportunity in the class—they knew ahead of time that they would receive a grade and written feedback about their work, and it was emphasized as an important milestone in the class. Here's what I wrote:

The narrative arc you used was not believable, and as a result, the presentation itself was poor. You left out steps in the story, making the story seem forced and unrealistic. Because it was unrealistic at the beginning, the rest of the story was questionable. This was particularly true on slides 1-10, where you set up the context for your product.

Specifically, when you discussed how a user would purchase your product, you didn't create a believable way that they would encounter the product in the first place. Instead, you simply said "The user bought the product." A way to improve this would be to start your story earlier; instead of beginning the narrative when the user is at the store, start the story when they first hear about the product from a friend or colleague. How did they hear about it? Why did their friends think to recommend it—what were the specific capabilities or qualities that the friends thought were worth talking about?

Compare the believability of the first part of your presentation with the end. You were successful in creating a story of an optimistic future when the user actually uses the product. We can empathize with the user because, on slides 11-15, you showed them slowly learning about the product. You spoke to their hesitations, and because you described how they only gradually received benefit from the product, it was more believable.

There are several parts of this feedback that make it effective.

- **Direct.** My feedback doesn't meander around the problems—it hits them dead on. I use an active tone, and say exactly what the student did well, and what they did poorly. For example, the first two sentences say *"The narrative arc you used was not believable, and as a result, the presentation itself was poor. You left out steps in the story, making the story seem forced and unrealistic."* This is different than "You could have done better on the story." The word "poor" is used on purpose—it's direct, and that directness is important. Now the student knows that something is wrong. That something is then explained: *"You left out steps in the story."* The student can pin-point what they need to change on future iterations. There's no ambiguity, and they don't have to try to interpret (often incorrectly) what I meant by my comments.

- **Specific.** The feedback is detailed and is tied to actual elements in the artifact the student has prepared, rather than talking only in general about what they made. For example, I reference specific sections of the presentation by slide number, I discuss specific statements in the presentation (*"You simply said..."*), and I ask specific questions about the content (*"How did they...? Why did they...? What were the...?"*)

- **Active.** The feedback emphasizes both things to do, and things not to do. The student can better compare the successful elements in their presentation with the ineffective ones, in order to better understand not just what didn't work but why it didn't work. This feedback is important because it helps short-circuit that peer-comparison described earlier. While I want students to learn from their peers, with this particular feedback, I don't want students judging what they did compared to what their colleagues did. I want them viewing their work in a more self-reflective manner.

- **Helpful.** The feedback is helpful. Instead of simply pointing out what was wrong, I also give suggestions on how to improve (*"A way to improve this would be..."*) It's not fair for a student to simply hear what they did wrong, because they won't be able to improve. By offering suggestions, students can compare what they did to what an expert feels would have been more productive or more valuable.

THE STRUCTURE OF FEEDBACK

Design isn't an objective field. There are better and worse design decisions, but not right and wrong decisions. In that subjectivity comes the importance of an expert. As the professor, it's unlikely that I'm an expert in the specific subject matter the student is exploring (for example, if a student is designing a banking application, it's unlikely that I'm an expert in banking apps). But I am an expert in the design process, and so I can offer expert feedback based on my experience. This is often subjective, and frequently delivered through a qualitative method (conversations or long written paragraphs).

But design can be assessed quantitatively, too, and while subjective, can be assessed consistently across students (what I sometimes call "subjective objectivity"). In these cases, I prepare a rubric that breaks down a comprehensive grade into smaller, more understandable and more piecemeal assessment opportunities and assign these point values.

For example, if I'm offering graded feedback on a design research report, I could simply give the entire report a grade of A-F and then offer written feedback. Or, I could take a more nuanced approach and break the feedback (and grade) into smaller pieces. I could individually assess:

- Was the report well written—did it have spelling or grammatical errors?

- Was the report well structured—did the contents flow in a way that was easy to understand?

- Was the methodology clear—can an audience understand what actions the student took?

- Were the findings in the report actionable—could someone take the findings and use them to make design changes?

I've now broken down an assessment into smaller, more digestible parts. I can grade each of these, perhaps giving each item 25 points instead of giving the whole assignment a single grade from 1-100. And, I could develop a more objective way of thinking about these point values. I might say that the most important part of the assignment was that the findings were actionable. So, I could give this part of the project a maximum of 70 points. This signals to the student that they should spend the most time on this part of the project. It also gives the professor more flexibility in grading—there's more fidelity and nuance within a 70 point range.

I'm of two minds about assigning point values to design work. Points help students (particularly less experienced students) understand how they are doing in a very clear, concise way. Larger points are indicative of better work; it's a very accessible way to understand progress. Points also add some level of continuity *across* students, so that grading becomes more fair. This helps the professor become more consistent when they are grading a large number of assignments.

But I've found that (not surprisingly) when given points, students tend to focus on the points rather than the qualitative feedback. Sometimes, those inexperienced students will argue for one or two more points, emphasizing that they disagree not with the substance of the assessment but only with the outcome.

Additionally, points add a very pragmatic structure around what is otherwise a very fuzzy subject matter. They "feel wrong" in the context of design—they imply that as the instructor, I have the right answer and some magic insight into what leads to student success.

I think the decision to assign point values depends on the context of the work. Assigning a "92" to a studio class seems incongruent with the organic nature of the course. But it may make more sense to have such a specific value when assessing a very particular skill, method, or set of facts—in a setting where students are practicing perspective drawing, for example, or where they are learning about the relationship between anatomy and human factors.

DELIVERY

It's tempting to wait until the student has completed an assignment or a task to communicate how they performed. This summary feedback is important to deliver. But, while this is easier and less time consuming than constant feedback, it lacks some of the effectiveness than continual "in the moment" reviews. This is because, at the end of the project, the decision making process and the critical thinking is over. Students will view the feedback in the context of what they made, rather than what they did. This means they can't course correct. They won't be able to improve the steps in their process, the decisions they make along the way, or the problem solving method selection criteria ("I used this method to solve that problem").

This puts a larger burden on the professor to work with students in a more direct, intimate capacity. To assess and redirect design effort in the moment means that I need to be there next to the student when they make decisions. In-class activities and studio courses act as the best context for this form of feedback, as they are contexts for *doing things*. But more intimate, one-on-one feedback requires more time with each student, and that means one of two things. Either I dedicate more time, overall, to the class, or there need to be less students. I keep my class sizes small so that I can focus on each student in more depth. Not all professors have that luxury, and that means that if they want to correct behavior in the moment, they'll need to spend more time in class and with the students.

Frequent feedback also means that I'm more intimately aware of what the student is doing, and that means I can be more detailed in my comments. Design decisions come fast and furious in the heart of the process, and if I only check in once a week, it's hard for me to really understand what students did and why they did it. More frequent feedback means I can be aware of those detailed decisions and can better understand the intent behind a student's actions.

I deliver grading feedback through both in-person (verbal) conversation and through written grading worksheets.

In-person feedback

In-person, verbal feedback provides an important opportunity for students to participate in a dialogue about their process, rather than a monologue. In a feedback session like this, I can deliver criticism about their process or their attitude and effort, and they can respond to help me understand why they are doing the things they are doing. Together, we can work through problems and come to solutions.

This in-person feedback can be delivered publicly in a group setting, or privately in a more one-on-one evaluation session. There are pros and cons to each. In a group setting, feedback can be delivered instantly. "In situ" feedback—delivering the feedback immediately and out loud—is one of the most effective ways of course-correcting negative behavior. This is because the actions that are most familiar (the most recent) are still active as episodic experiences: they still have "color" to their details, rather than fading into generalities. More direct feedback can be offered immediately, and as we've seen above, that directness is important for students to learn.

On the other hand, public feedback can be embarrassing for a student, and they may ignore the feedback and instead focus only on the fact that they did something they perceive as wrong. This is a miseducative experience: there is no learning happening, only shaming.

Private feedback is delayed, and that means that I need to be more proactive in remembering the details of the learning situation. I need to take better notes so that I can offer nuanced evaluation even after the fact. However, this form of feedback is helpful for students to privately internalize what they need to improve. They can focus on the skills or concepts themselves, instead of being overwhelmed with their own feelings.

Public and private in-person feedback is about trust. Early in their educational journey, I haven't established the trust of students, and so public feedback feels less fair—students don't understand that my criticism is coming from a place of respect, and so they are more likely to ignore the substance of the feedback and focus only on the emotion of it. Later in the quarter, when I have established the respect and trust of the group, public feedback is more likely to resonate and feel appropriate.

Written feedback

Written feedback is valuable too, but rarer in design contexts (perhaps design professors don't like to write!) Written feedback sheets are artifacts that, like any design artifacts, put stakes in the ground. They say "this, but not that" in a way that's memorable, because students can refer to the written feedback over and over. Written feedback also gives me a chance to compose my thoughts more thoroughly. I can be much more detailed, and instead of simply providing feedback on an artifact, I can better prepare feedback on attitude, approach, and teamwork. This means I can offer more complicated, more nuanced, and more thoughtful responses with the benefit of my own reflection.

When I write feedback, I often find myself writing similar comments for each student. I'll leverage both custom writing per student, and also common writing. I'll create a series of statements and copy/paste them for each student. This isn't lazy grading—it's common that students at a similar place in the curriculum will benefit from the same feedback. But it's important to offer a balance of comments that are widely applicable, and comments that are unique to each student; the personalized nature of feedback makes it more likely that a student will hear and integrate that feedback into their process.

I use written evaluation when students have completed a large or important milestone in their learning—often, the end of a project or the creation of an artifact. This gives me something concrete to use to assess their skill or knowledge acquisition. I can focus on the learning outcomes and compare them to the work product, and be as objective as possible in offering ways to improve. I'll write personalized comments (often 1000 words or more) to help students reflect on the previous 8 weeks. These comments typically include:

- **A reflection on comprehensive skills learned**. I'll describe the skills that I expected the student to learn, and then describe the progress I observed. For example, I may explain to students that I saw them gain competency in sketching, evidenced by their improved use of perspective and line weight. This is a broad statement; it isn't referring to any specific assignment or project, but instead, to a generalizable outcome. We defined these outcomes when we designed the class; this one may have been "The student will sketch accurately in perspective." By comparing their work to the outcome, I help the student see how the course was valuable to them.

- **Comments on attitude and approach**. It's helpful for students to see, in writing, descriptions of behavior that's both good and bad. For example, if a student is having trouble working with their team—and has had trouble working with their team for the entire quarter—this is an opportunity for me to help them see that the behavior is sustained.

I might write something like "*I consistently observed that you were 'separate' from your team. In many studio classes, you sat on the edge of the room and didn't participate on our discussion. For example, during our last session, you did not actively participate in our discussion about perspective sketching. As a result of this behavior, your team suffered—they were left to guess what you were thinking, and they didn't benefit from your contributions. In the future, I would like to see you better participate by speaking more frequently, sketching on the whiteboard, and sitting closer to the group."*

This comment is specific, referencing continual behavior. If this behavior was a one-off, I would have been able to correct it during the specific studio session; but, in final feedback, my goal is to show patterns to students.

- **Positive reflection**. An academic milestone should have room for positivity, too. I'll be sure to include comments about how I see the student performing in the future. I may write something like *"I'm excited to see how you progress through the next quarter, as you apply what you've learned related to sketching in perspective in your future assignments."* While not overly celebratory, this encourages the student to apply what they've learned and ends the quarter on a strong note, even if the student's performance was not as productive as it should have been.

Expert-based feedback

In addition to in-person feedback and written feedback, I'll also bring in experts to offer evaluation and help students see where they can improve: I invite working practitioners to class. Because they have deep expertise in design, they can offer detailed, supportive, and believable suggestions. And because they are a neutral third party, I've found that students tend to really listen to and react to their feedback.

I think this is because they come with an aura of respect based on where they work and what they've done. If I bring in a creative director from a famous consultancy like frog or IDEO, students value their opinion implicitly because they value that particular company's work. Sometimes to my bemusement, the visiting expert can say exactly what I've been saying, but students are more likely to listen to them!

Conclusion

I've shared with you the things I've learned in my fifteen years of teaching. These are things I wish someone had told me when I started.

I didn't spend time talking about some other issues facing design educators, but I've written a lot about those in other places. Some of these topics include the role of online learning, the relationship between design and computer science, design portfolios, wicked problems in design, and the nature of scale in higher education. You can learn about some of these topics at my personal site, http://www.jonkolko.com

I also want to share some resources that you may find useful.

Austin Center for Design has published a free book on the nature of Wicked Problems in design. The book covers topics of ethical design—of selecting problems that are worth solving. http://bit.ly/wickedproblemsbook

Austin Center for Design also regularly updates a free design library of content that you can repurpose in your classes. These lectures are the same content we use at the school. http://bit.ly/ac4dlibrary

FINAL THOUGHTS

The design studio is a wonderful environment for creativity. It's a place, and a vibe, and a process: it becomes the backdrop for meaningful experiential learning. Inside of the design studio, classes are built around learning outcomes and a thoughtful timeline of learning interventions. Students learn skills focused on ethnographic research, synthesizing complexity into meaningful insights, shaping services and products, and evaluating their work to ensure it is usable and useful.

Fundamental to this learning is critique, a unique form of assessment that helps ideas advance. Constant presentation helps students gain confidence in their process and their own abilities. Dialogue around theory helps them build a perspective on the role of design in the world around them.

Students practice their work through assignments, iterating, testing, and refining their ideas. They develop craft by practicing methods, and they get constant and regular feedback through in-person and written grading. And they build confidence and thoughtfulness as they receive targeted assessments.

Many of these things are simple and obvious (although, at least for me, they were only obvious in retrospect). I've found that there aren't any tricks to teaching effectively. It's hard work. But I've shared methods and techniques that help design students learn and grow.

I see my graduates doing great things after I teach them using the processes I've described here. Methodical, thoughtful and respectful design education helps students become methodical, thoughtful and respected design professionals.

Design is one of the most powerful forces we have in changing the world around us. It shapes culture and changes the way we interact with one-another. We can't leave design education to chance, because our graduates will soon be in charge of building the designed world around us.

About the Author

Jon is a Partner at Modernist Studio, and the Founder of Austin Center for Design. He was previously the Vice President of Design at Blackboard, the largest educational software company in the world. He joined Blackboard with the acquisition of MyEdu, a startup focused on helping students succeed in college and get jobs.

Jon has also held the positions of Executive Director of Design Strategy at Thinktiv, a venture accelerator in Austin, Texas, and both Principal Designer and Associate Creative Director at frog design, a global innovation firm. He has been a Professor of Interaction and Industrial Design at the Savannah College of Art and Design, where he was instrumental in building both the Interaction and Industrial Design undergraduate and graduate programs.

Jon has also held the role of Director for the Interaction Design Association (IxDA), and Editor-in-Chief of interactions magazine, published by the ACM. He is regularly asked to participate in high-profile conferences and judged design events, including the 2013 Cooper-Hewitt National Design Awards. He has taught at the University of Texas at Austin, the

Center for Design Studies of Monterrey, in Mexico, and Malmö University, in Sweden.

Jon is the author of five books:

- **Thoughts on Interaction Design,** published by Morgan Kaufmann,

- **Exposing the Magic of Design: A Practitioner's Guide to the Methods and Theory of Synthesis,** published by Oxford University Press,

- **Wicked Problems: Problems Worth Solving,** published by Austin Center for Design,

- **Well Designed: How to use Empathy to Create Products People Love,** published by Harvard Business Review Press, and

- **Creative Clarity,** published by Brown Bear Press.

www.ingramcontent.com/pod-product-compliance
Lightning Source LLC
Chambersburg PA
CBHW072144170526
45158CB00004BA/1506